AF386031

ALL THAT
HEAVEN
ALLOWS

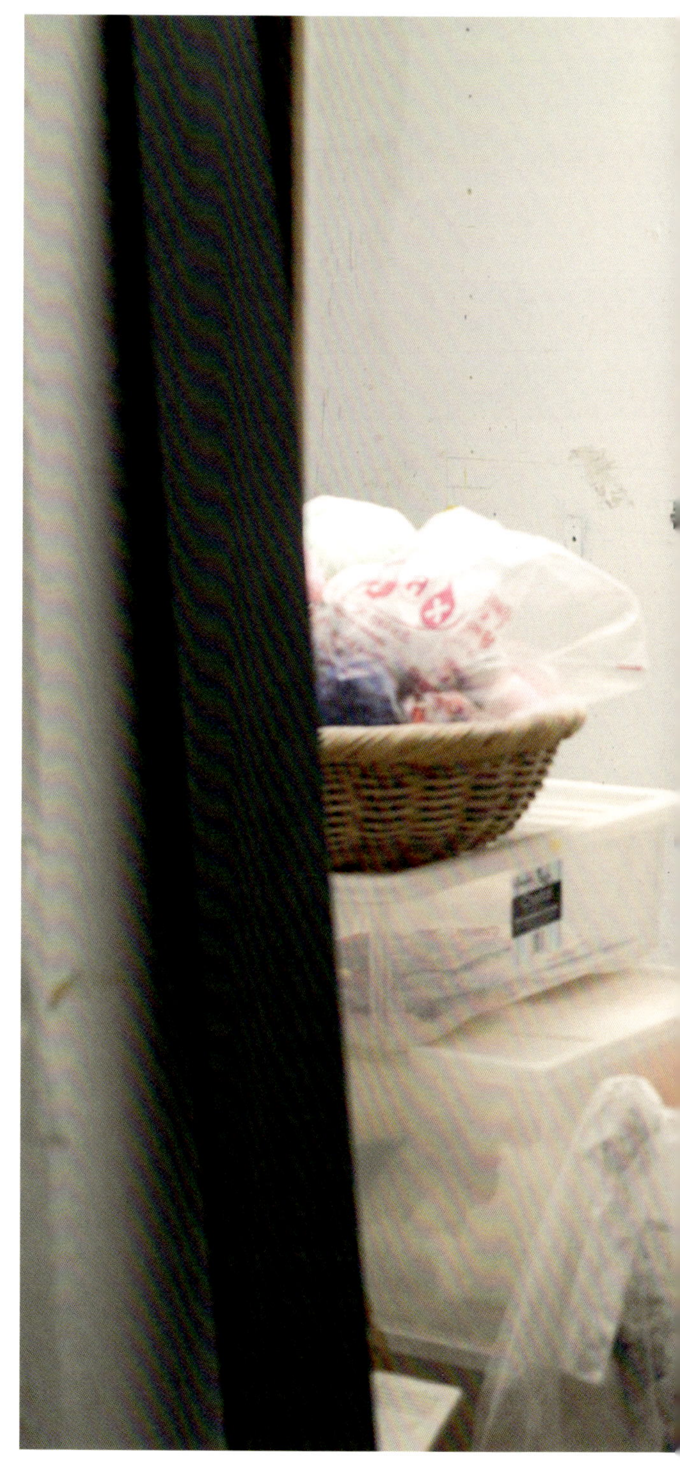

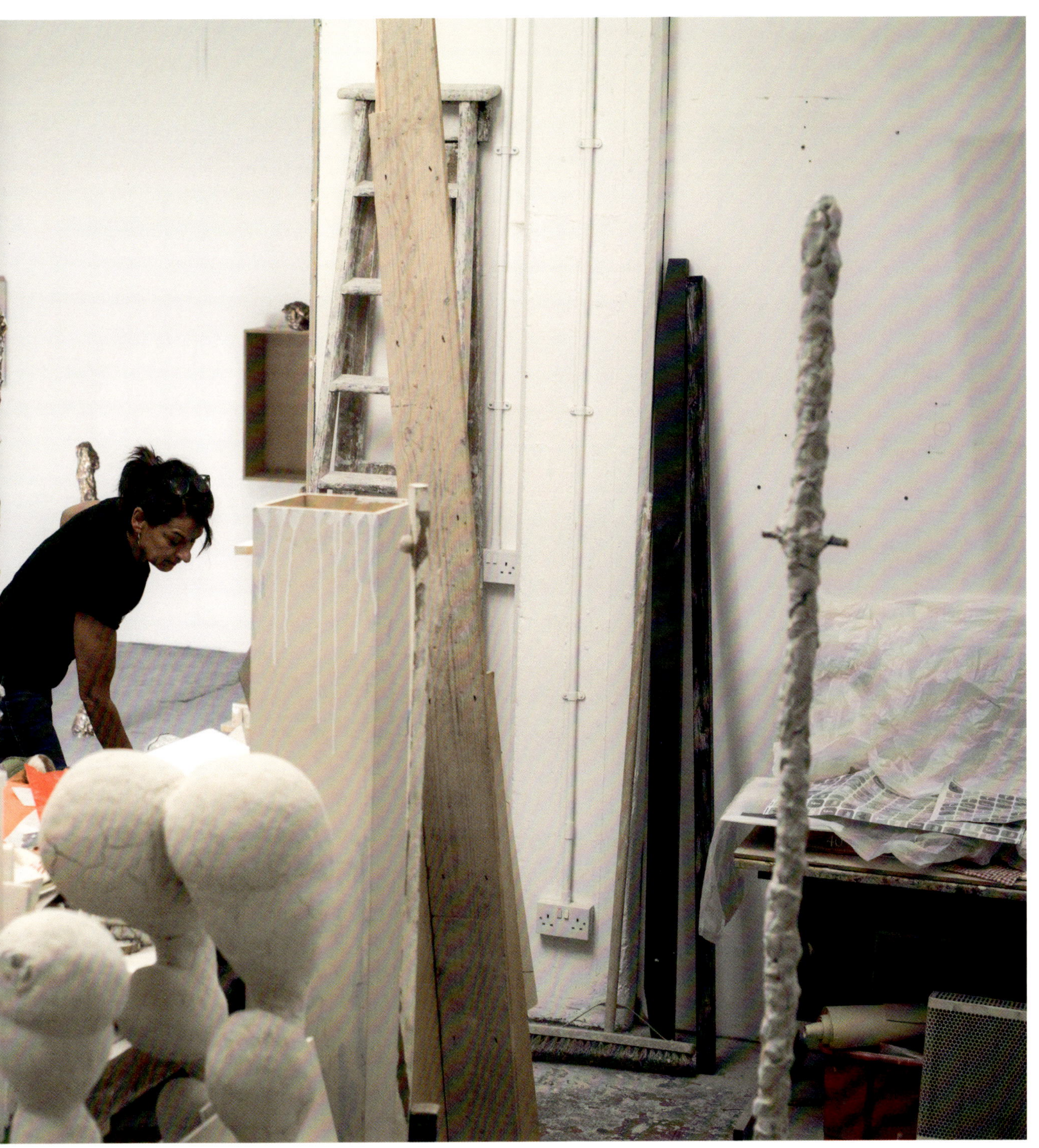

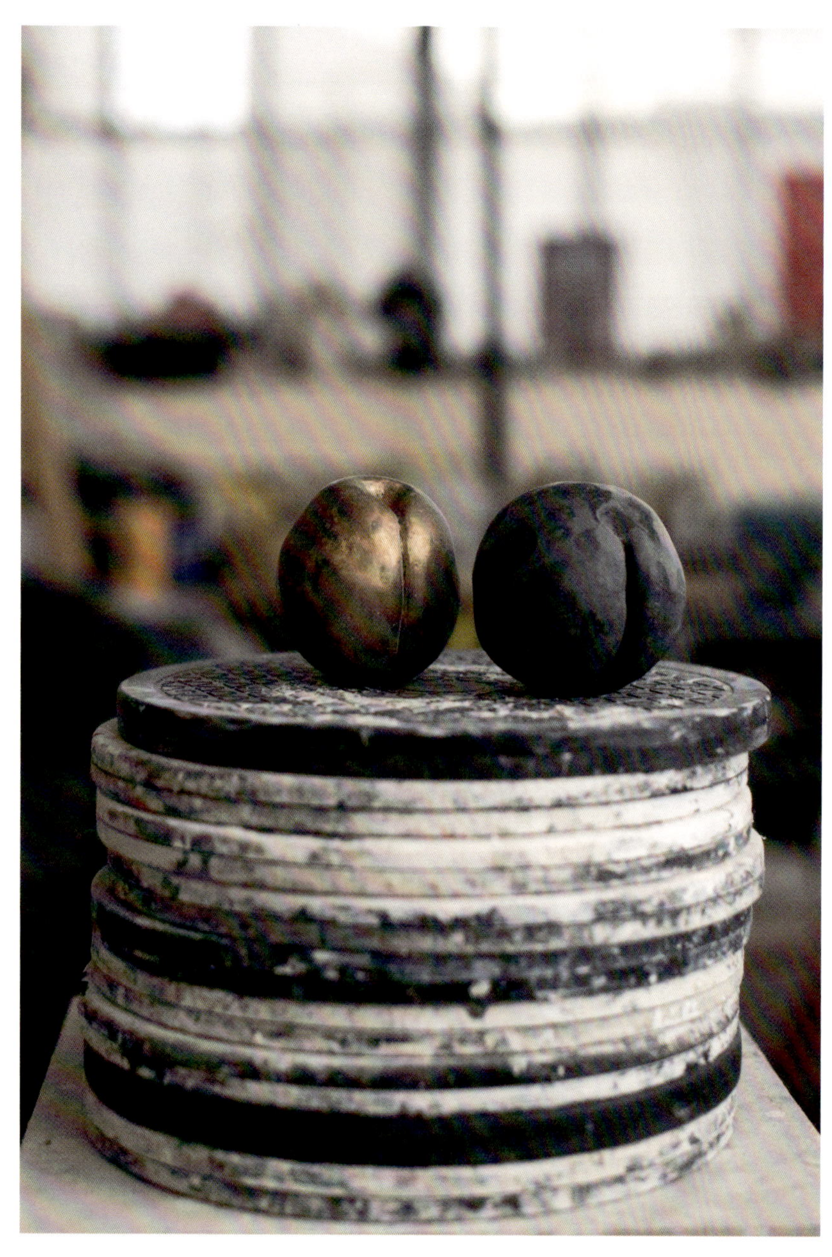

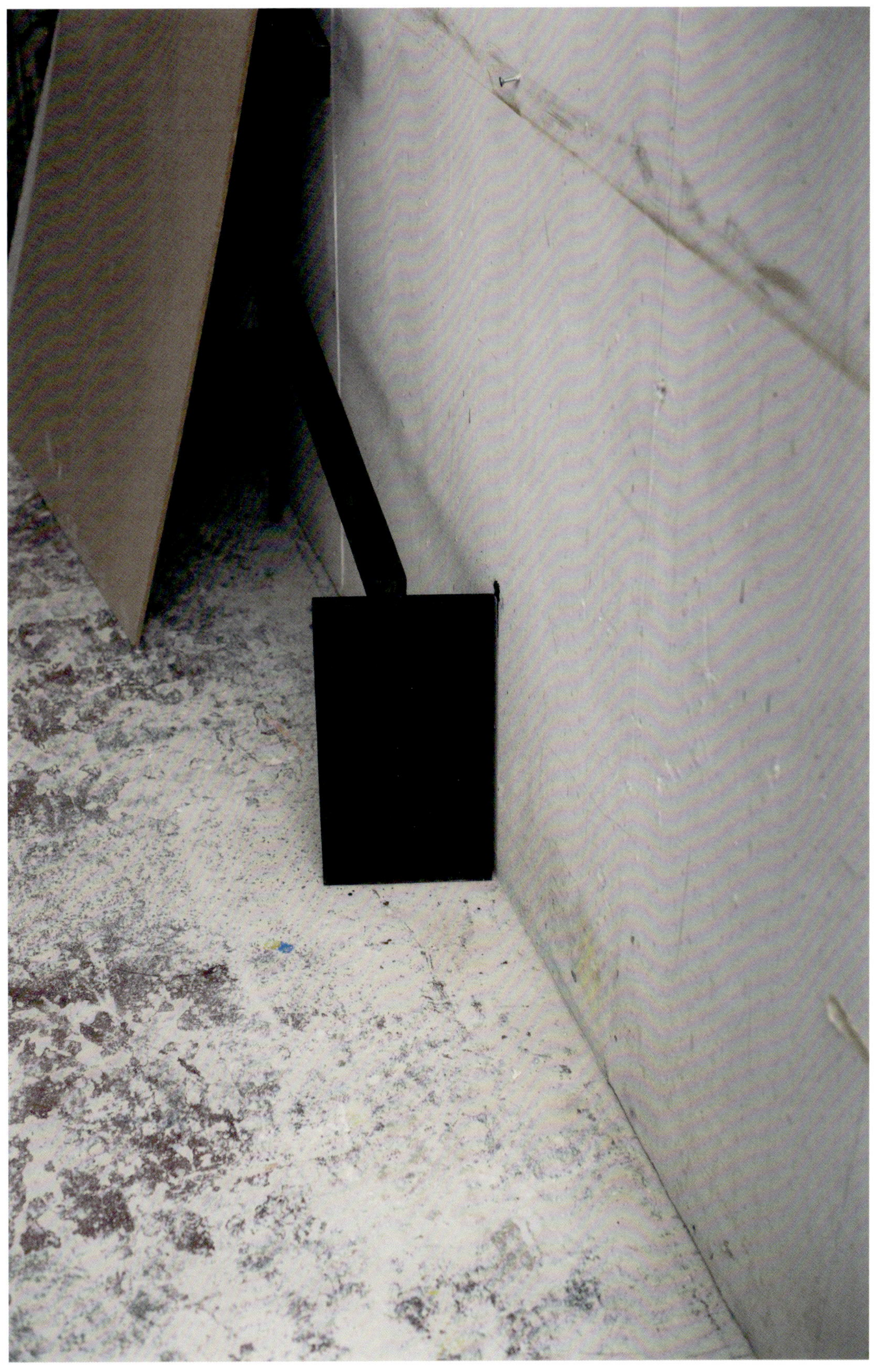

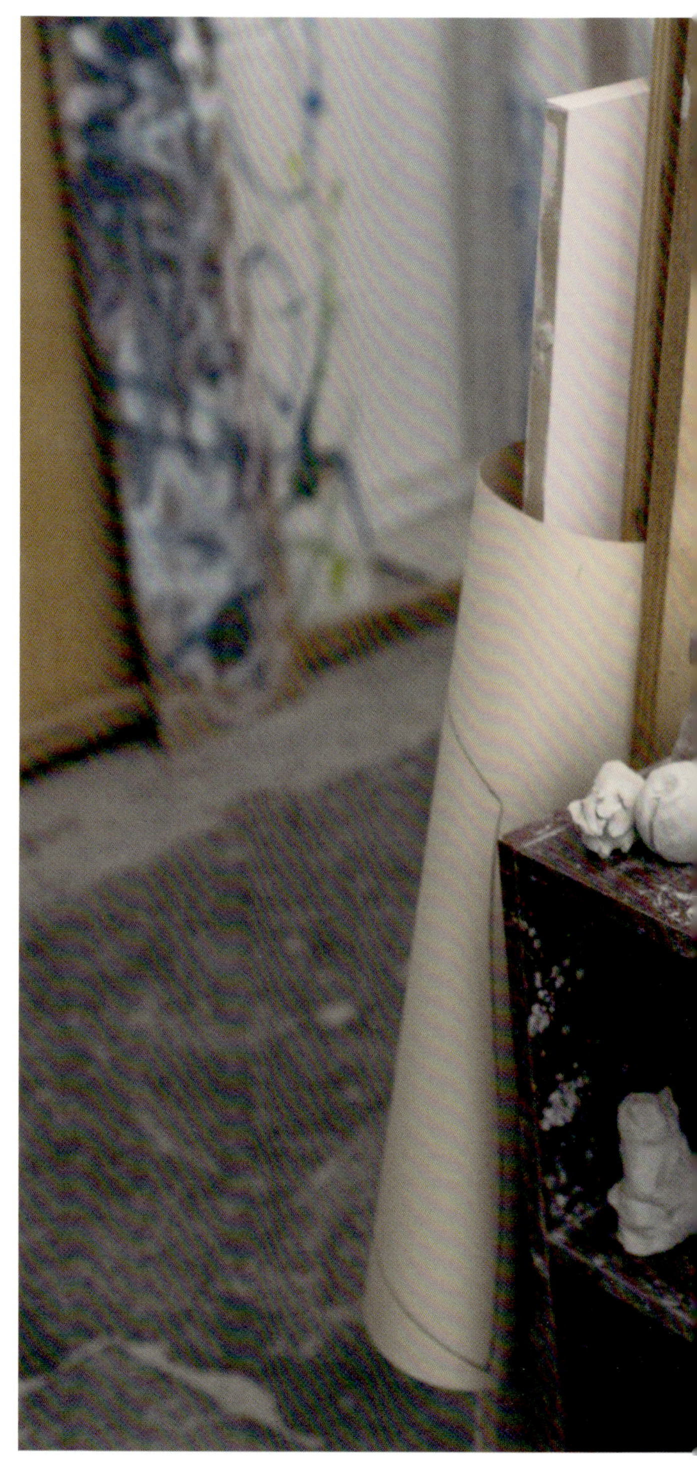

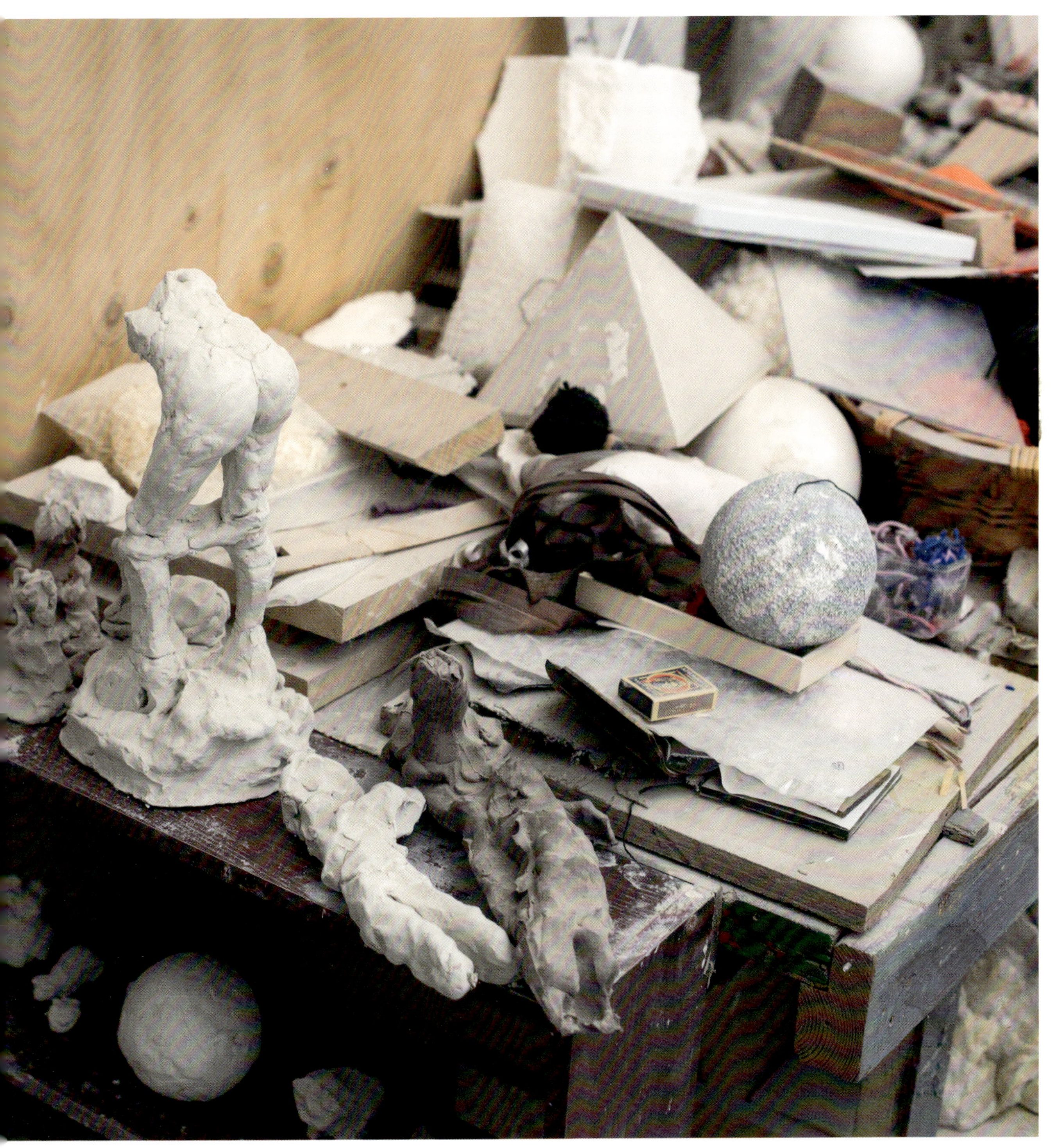

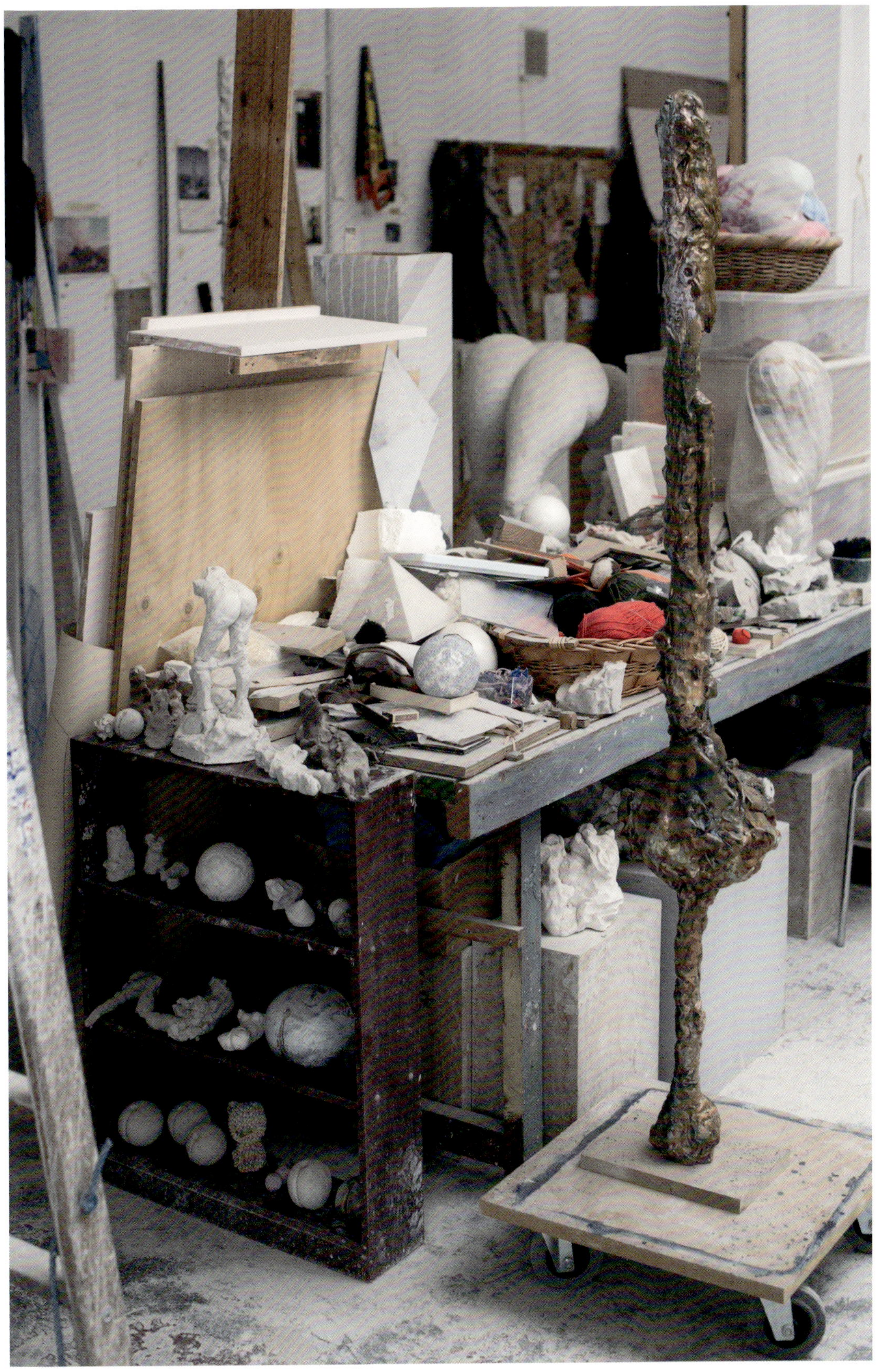

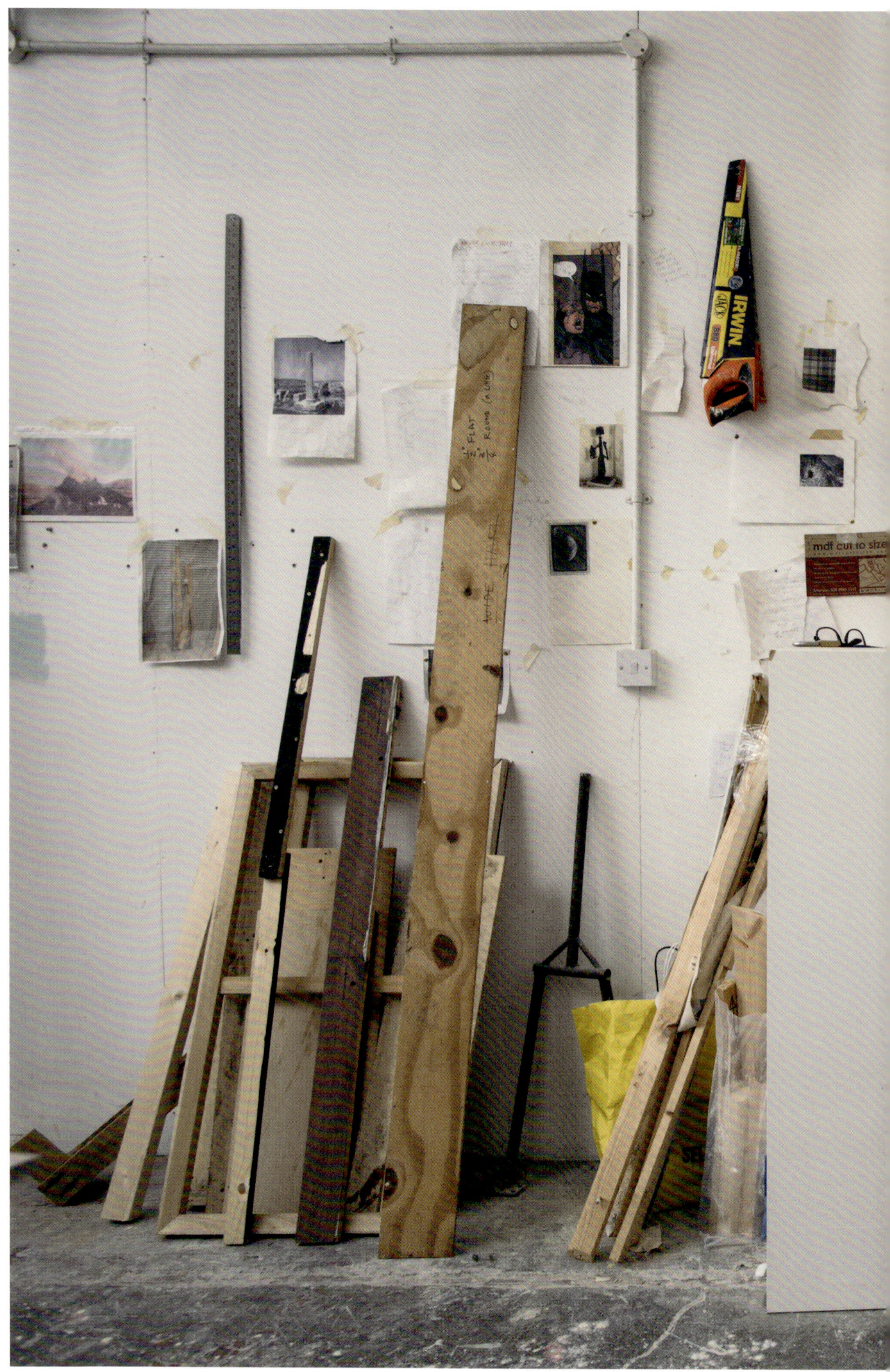

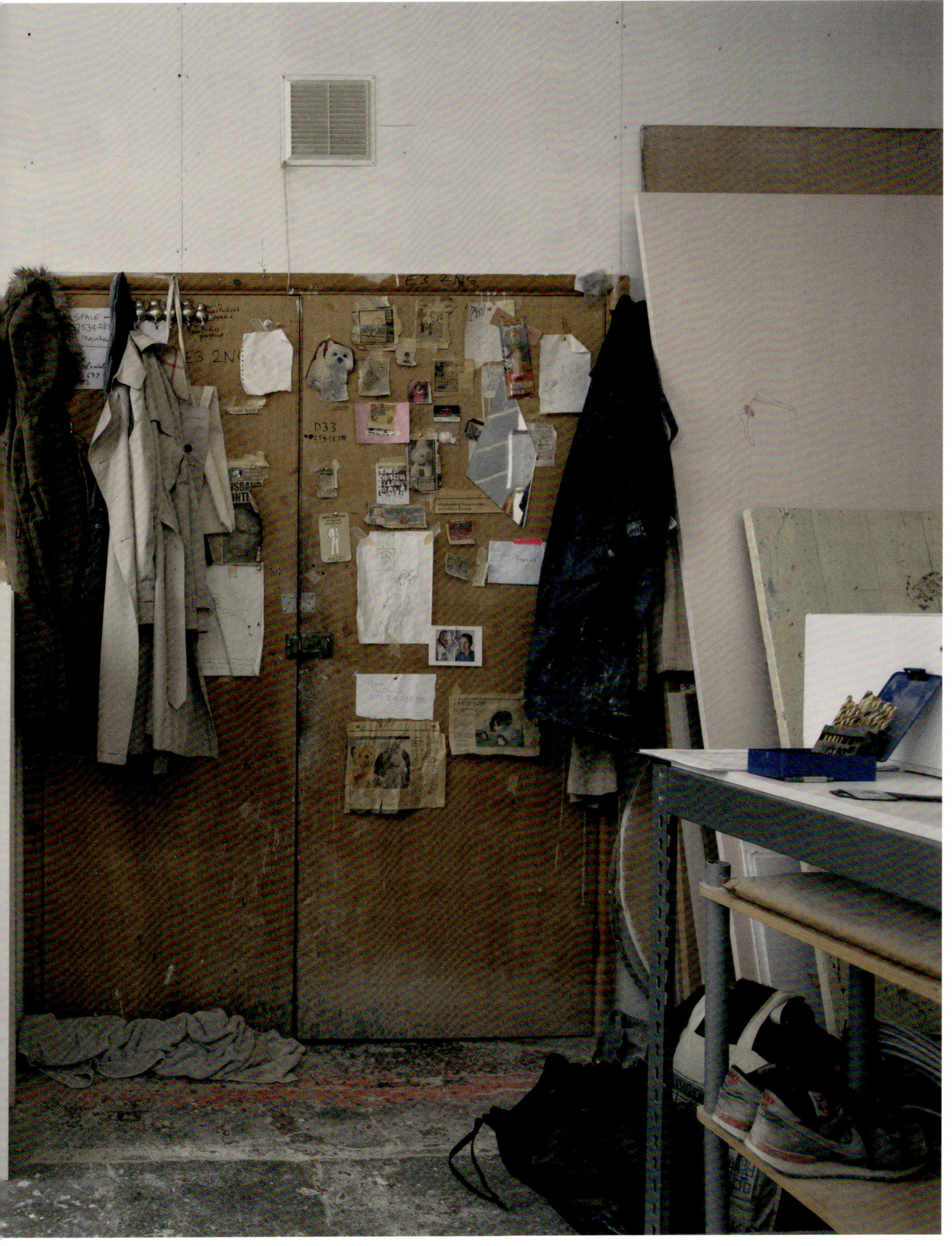

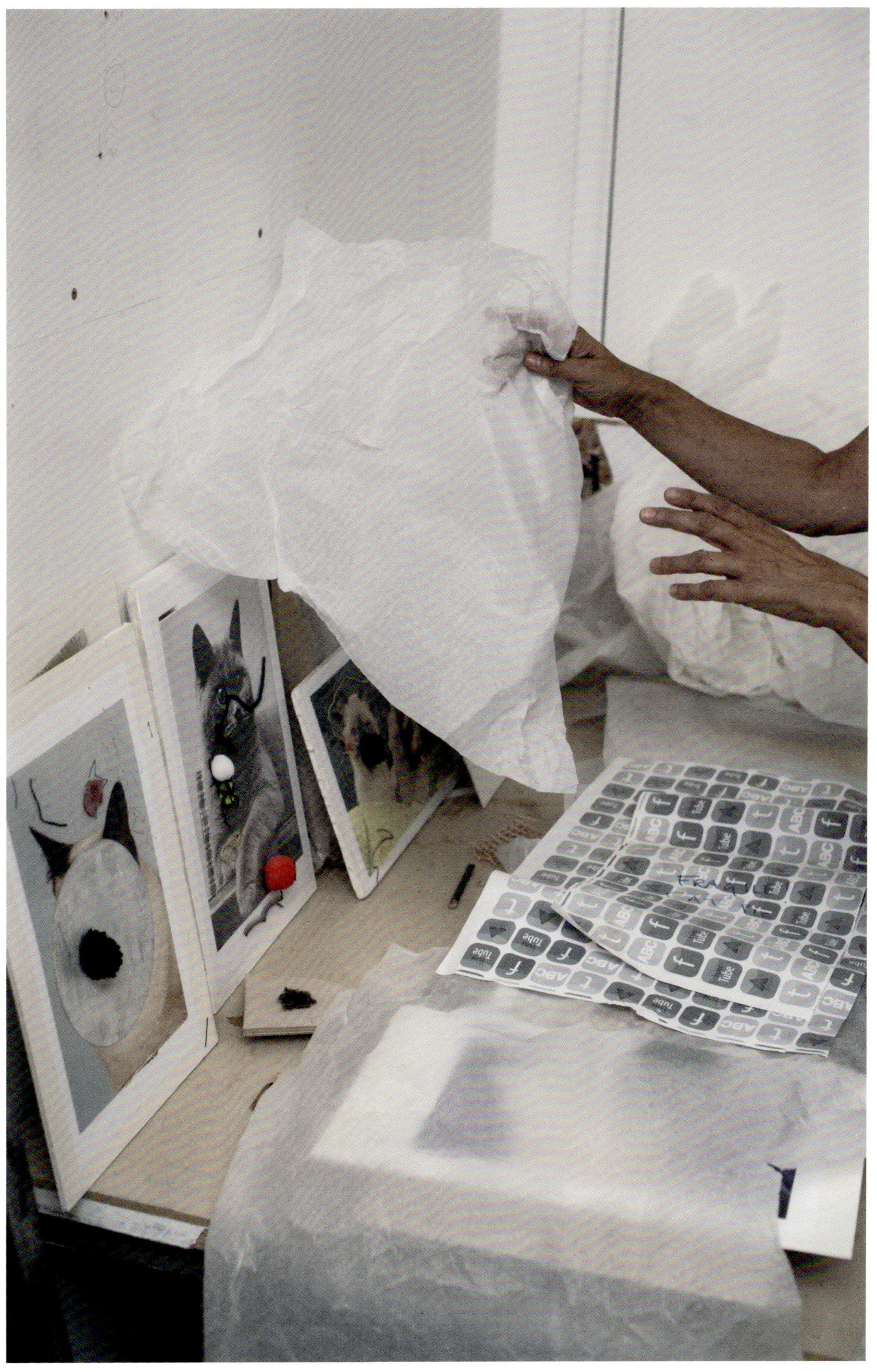

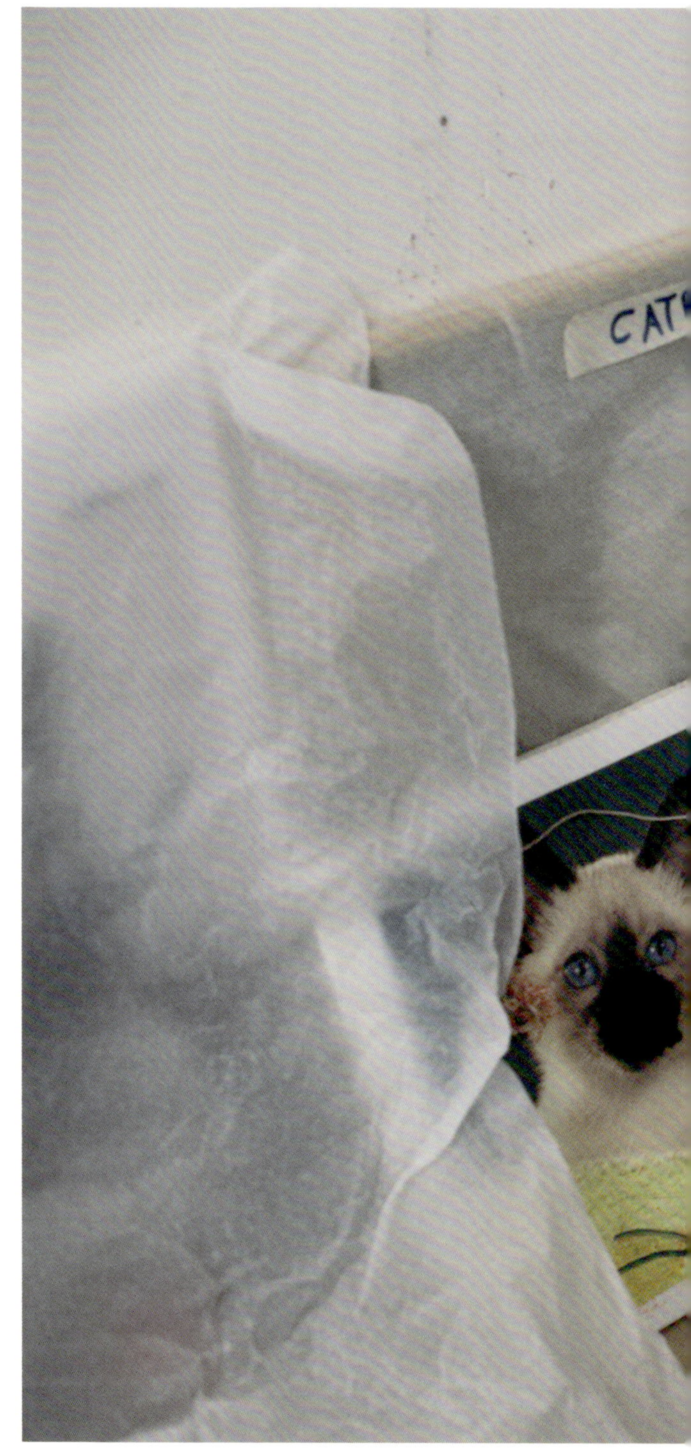
CAT

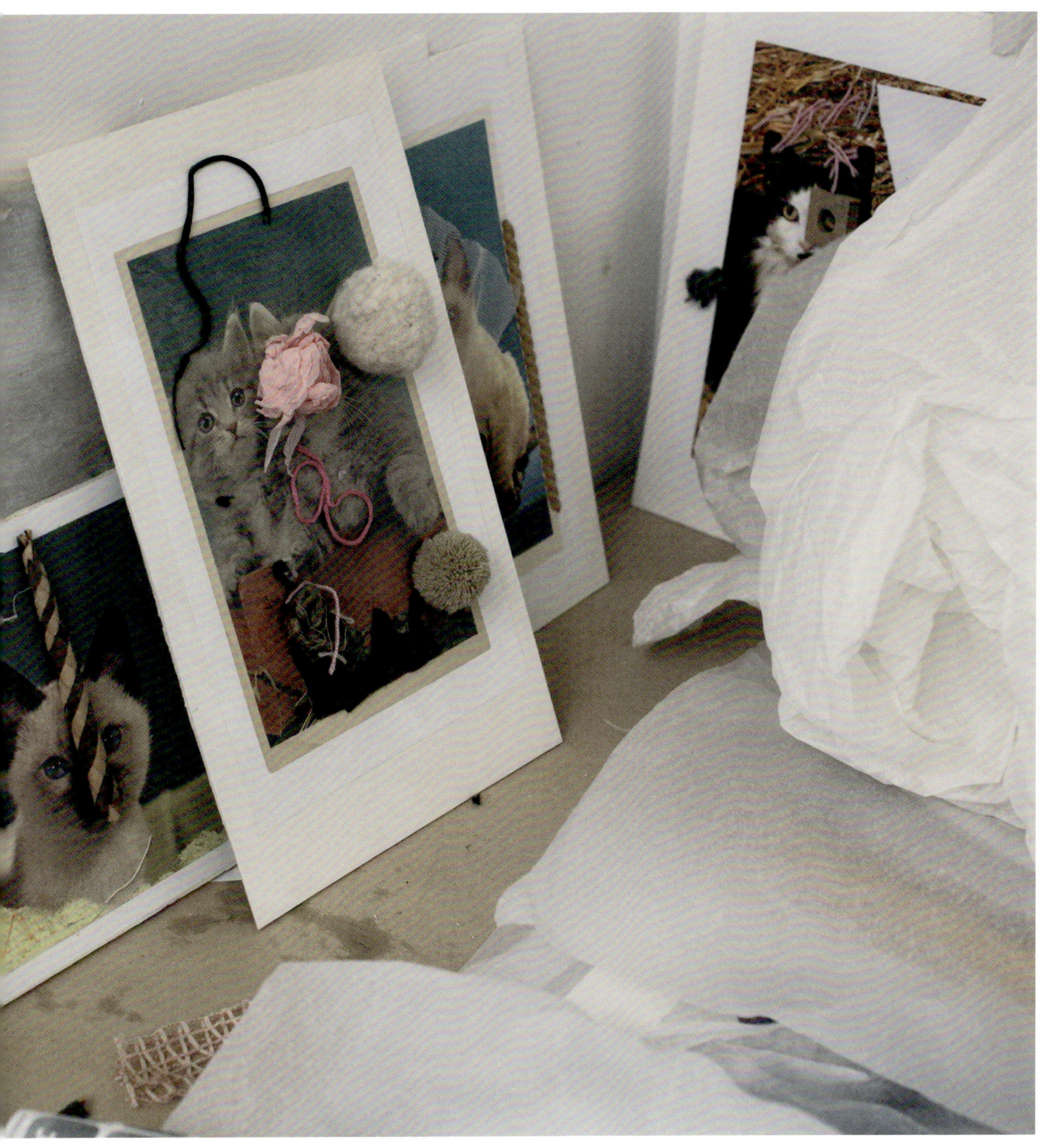

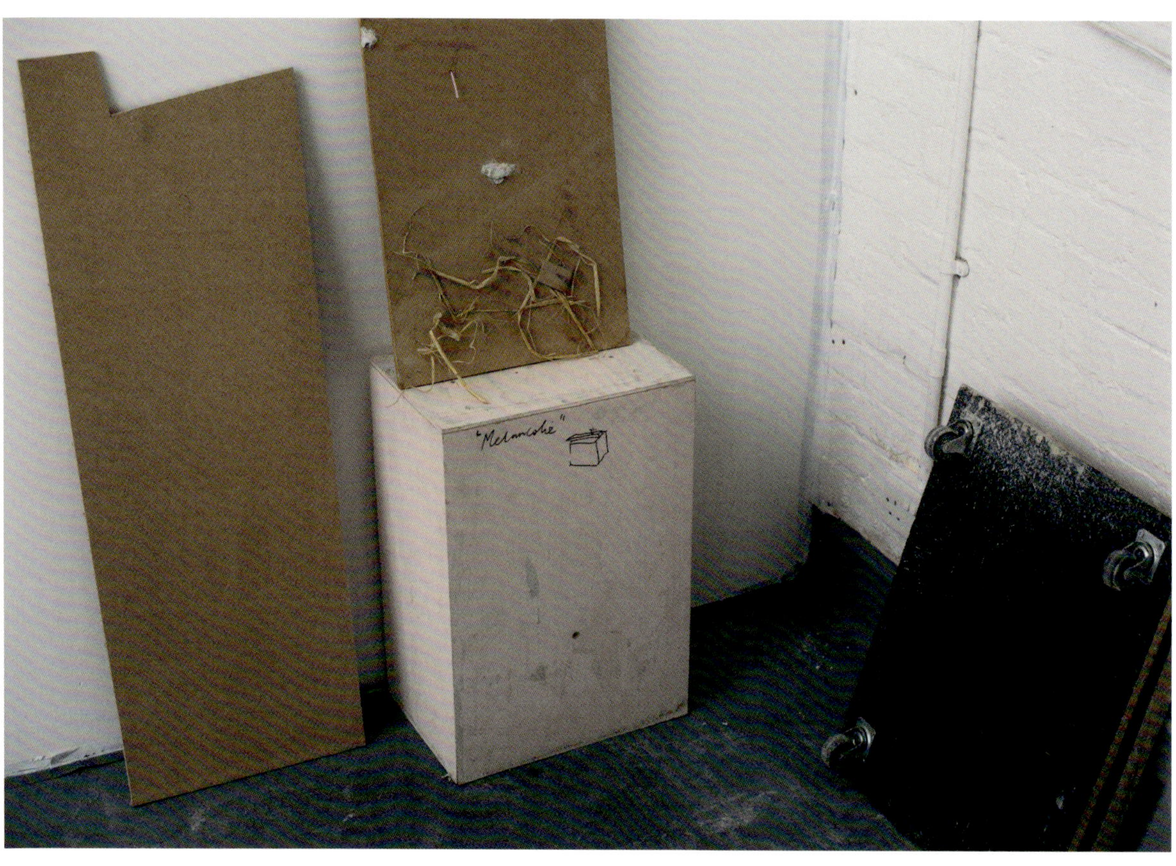

"Melancolie"

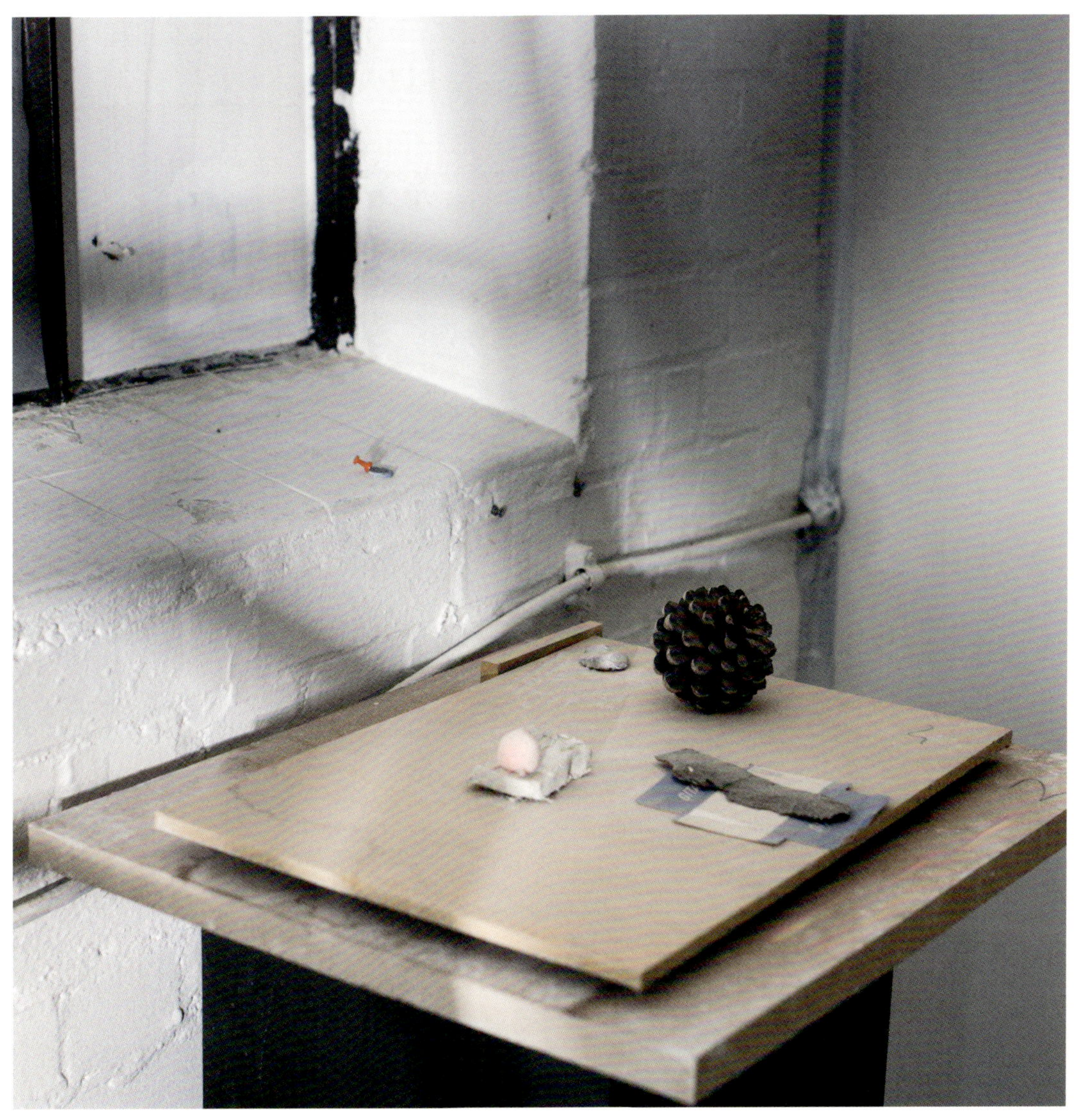

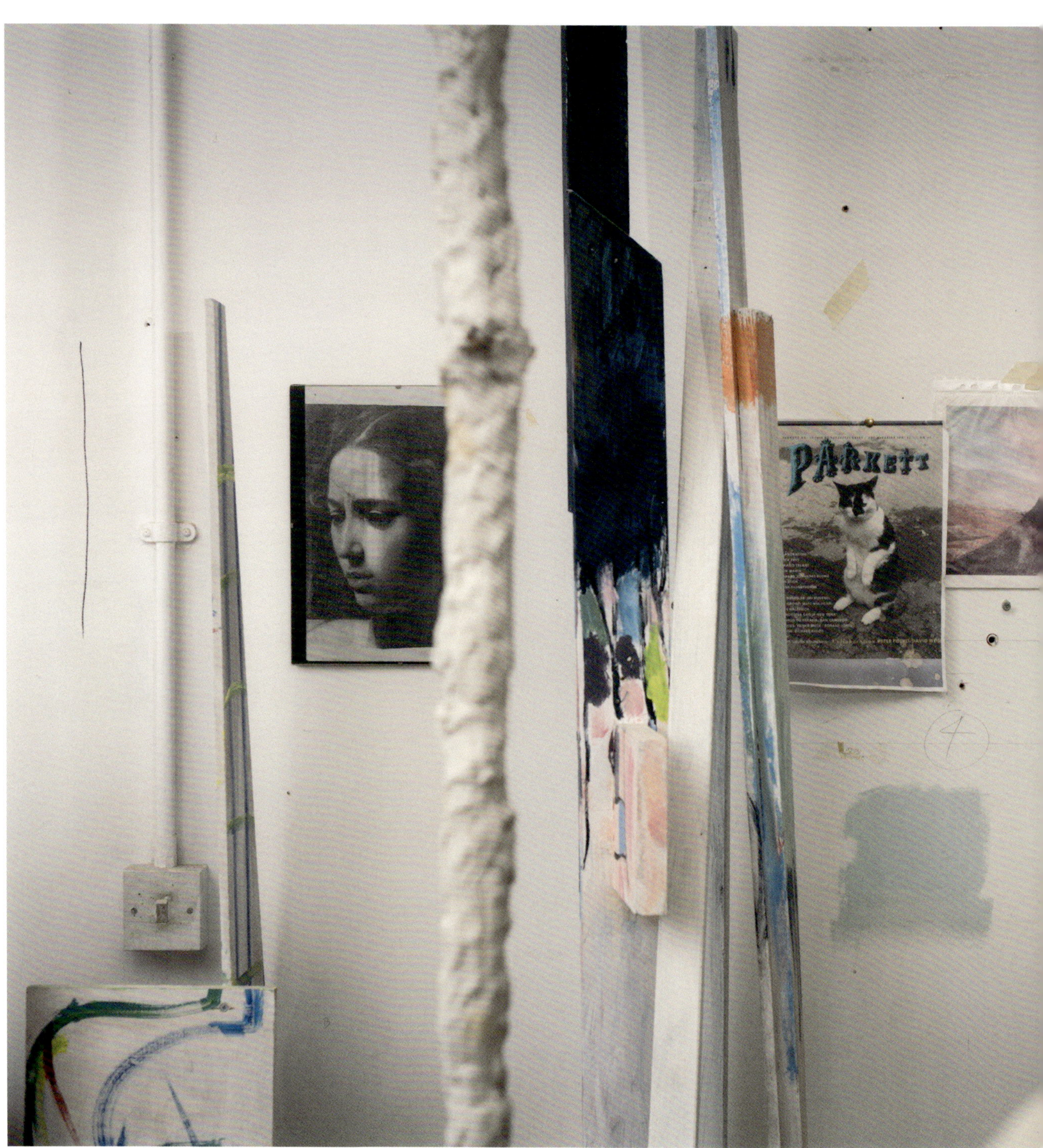
PARKETT

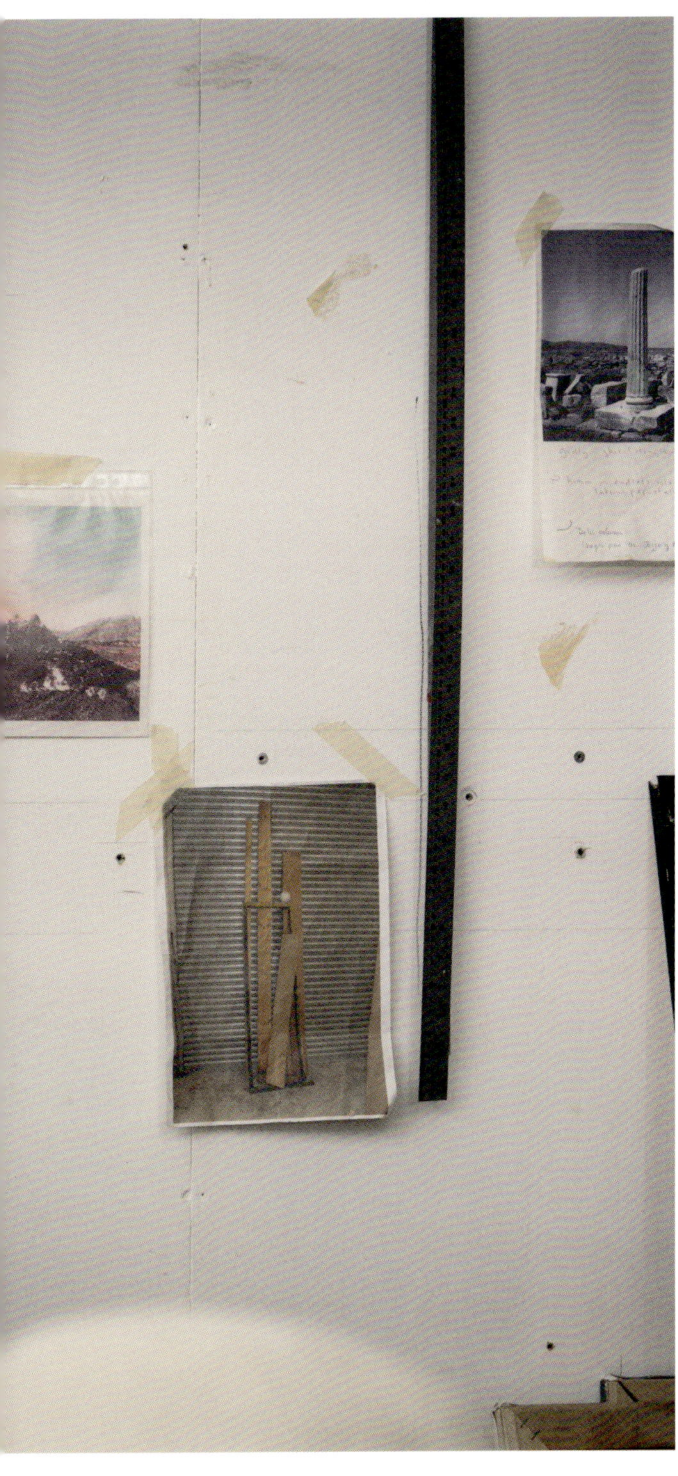

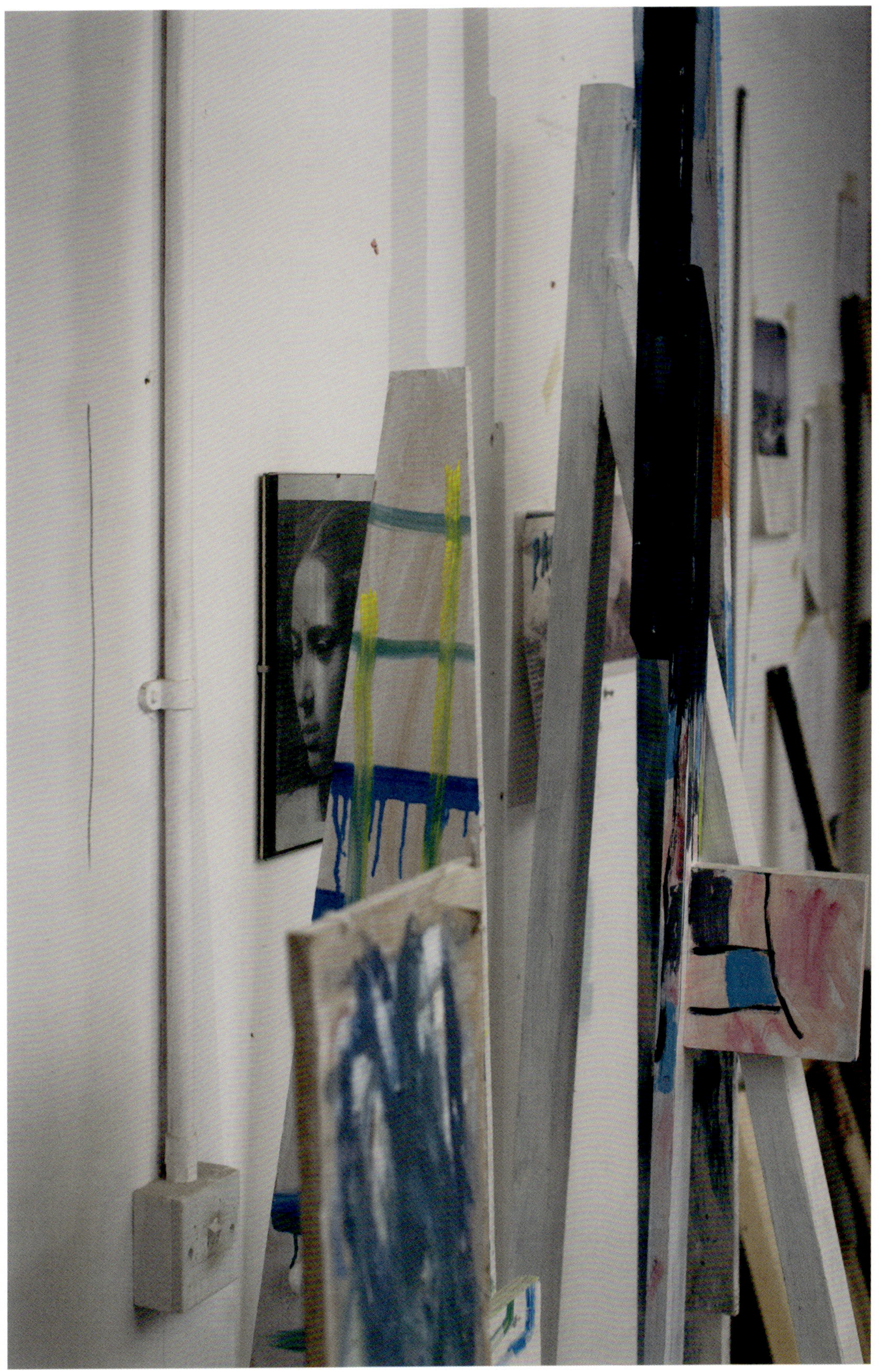

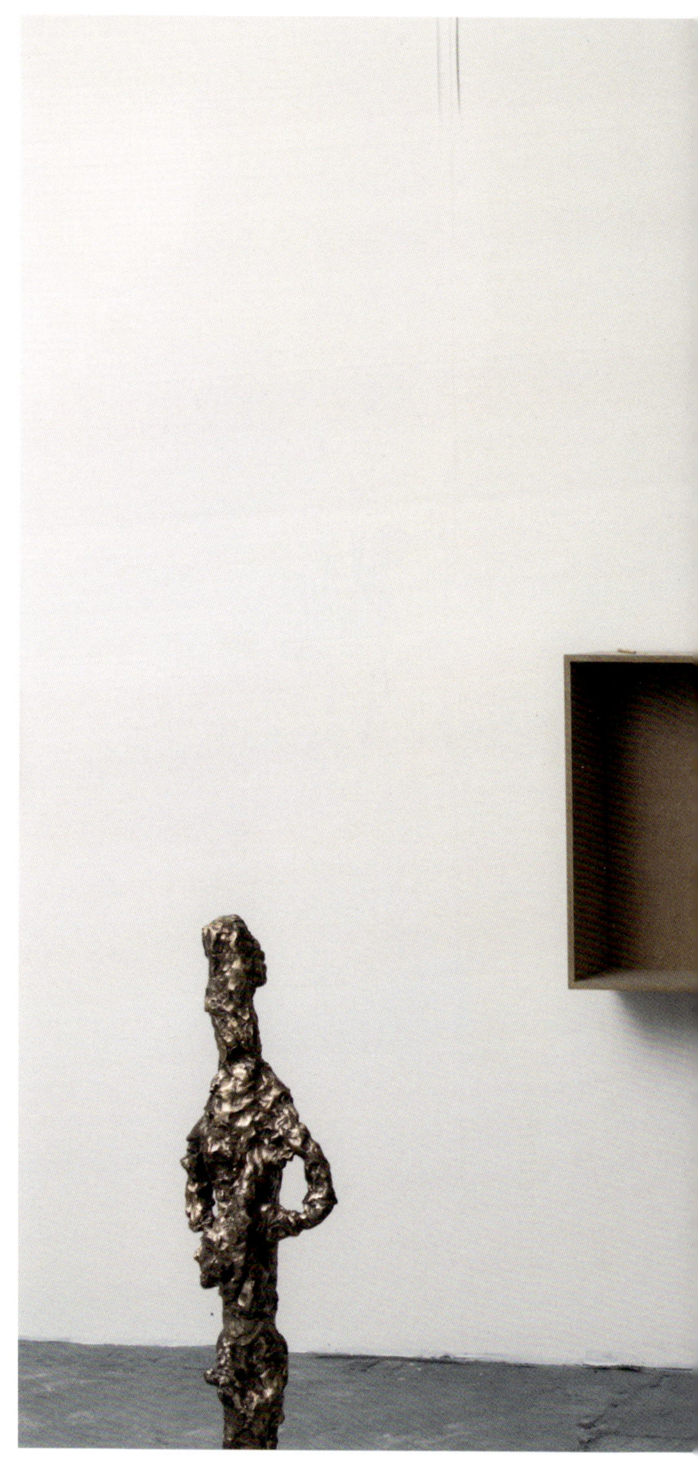

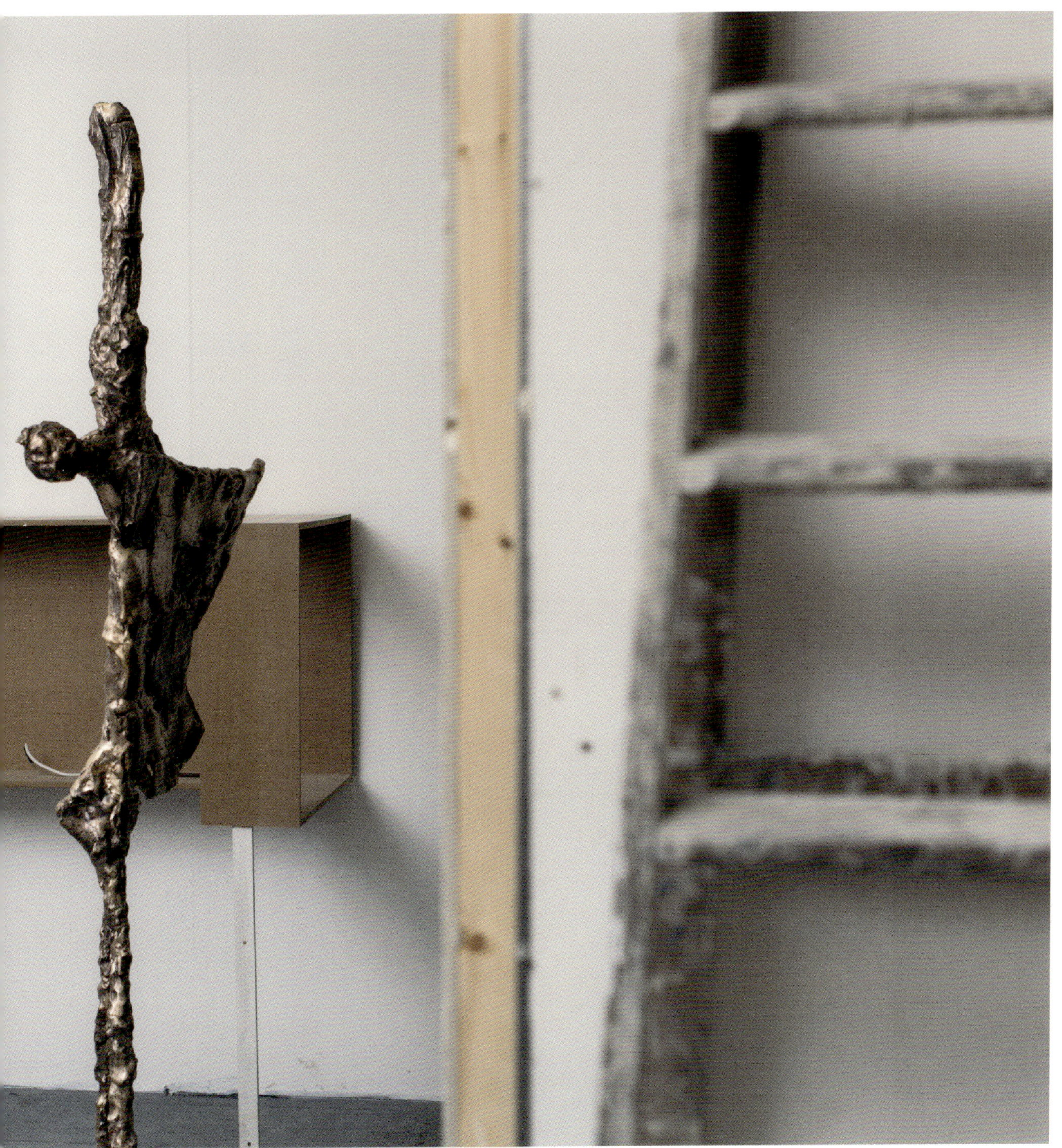

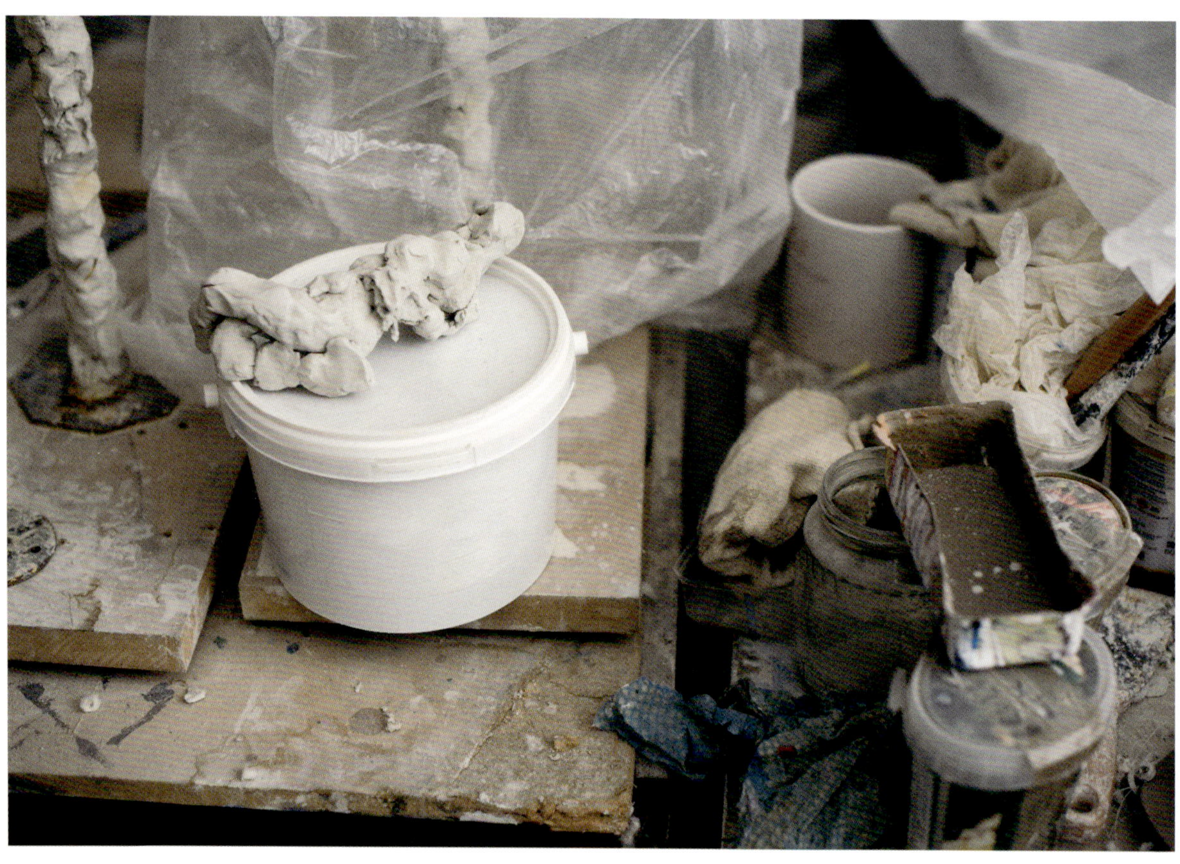

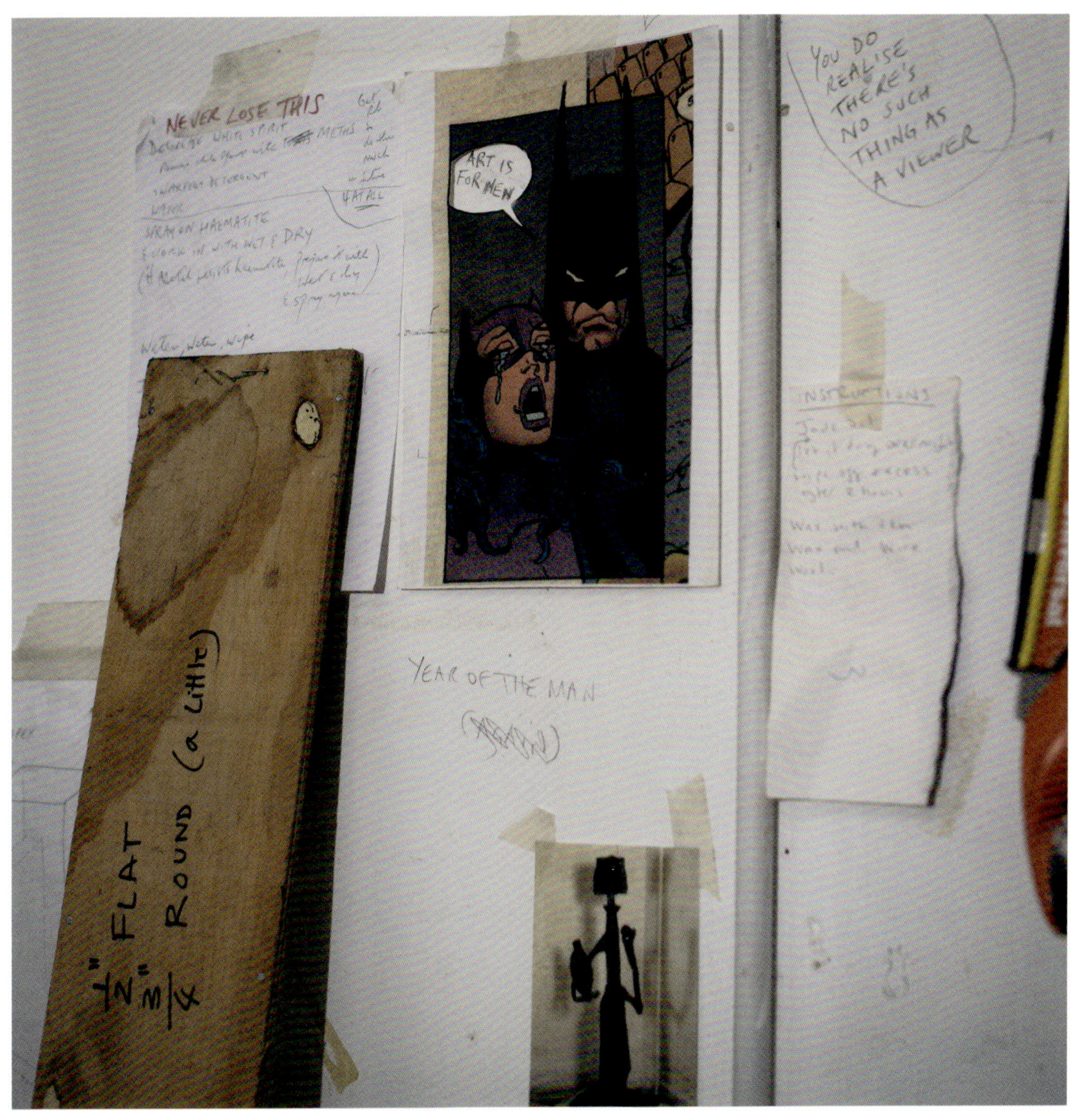

NEVER LOSE THIS
ART IS FOR MEN
YOU DO REALISE THERE'S NO SUCH THING AS A VIEWER
INSTRUCTIONS
YEAR OF THE MAN
(AGAIN)
½" FLAT
3/4" ROUND (a little)

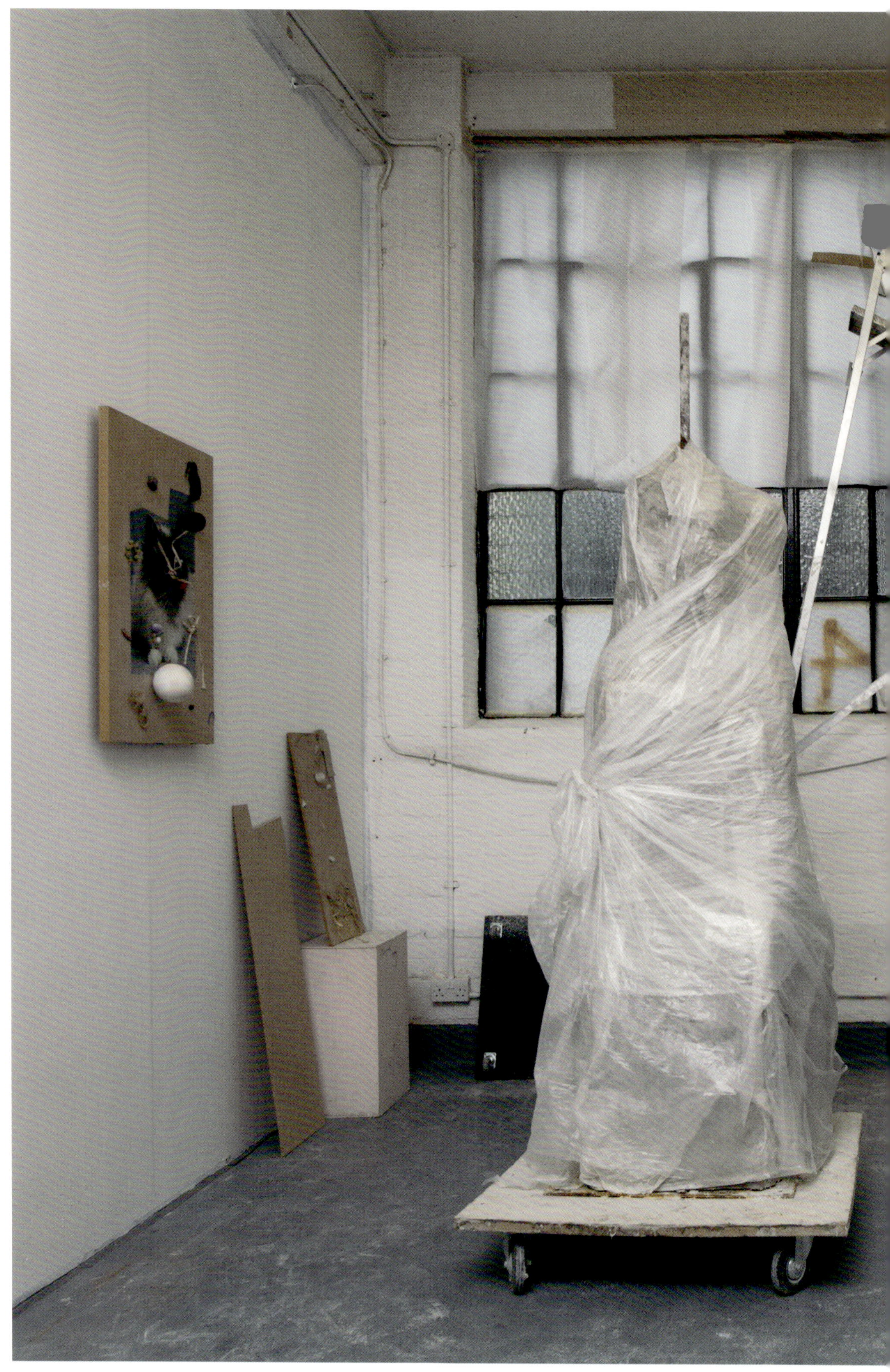

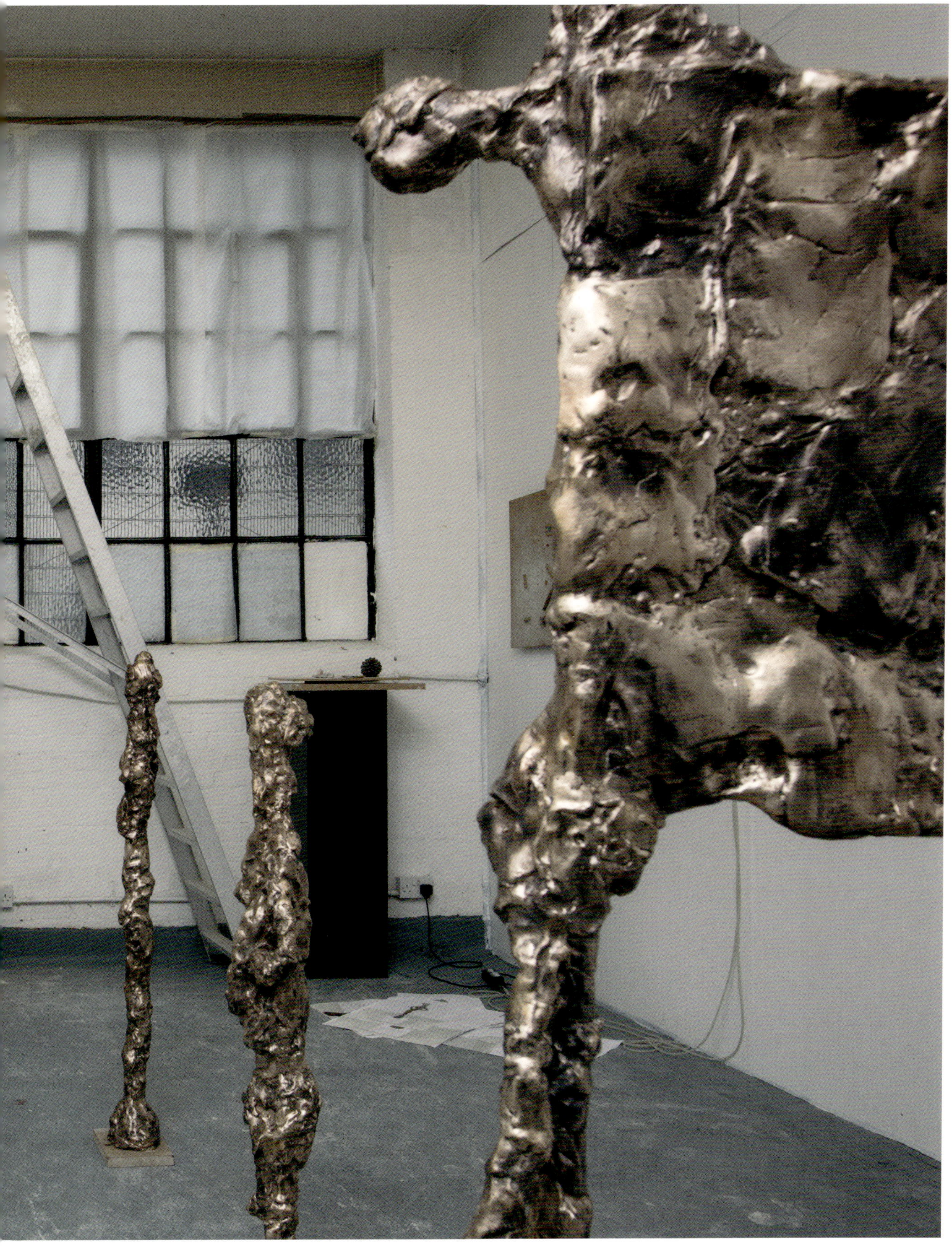

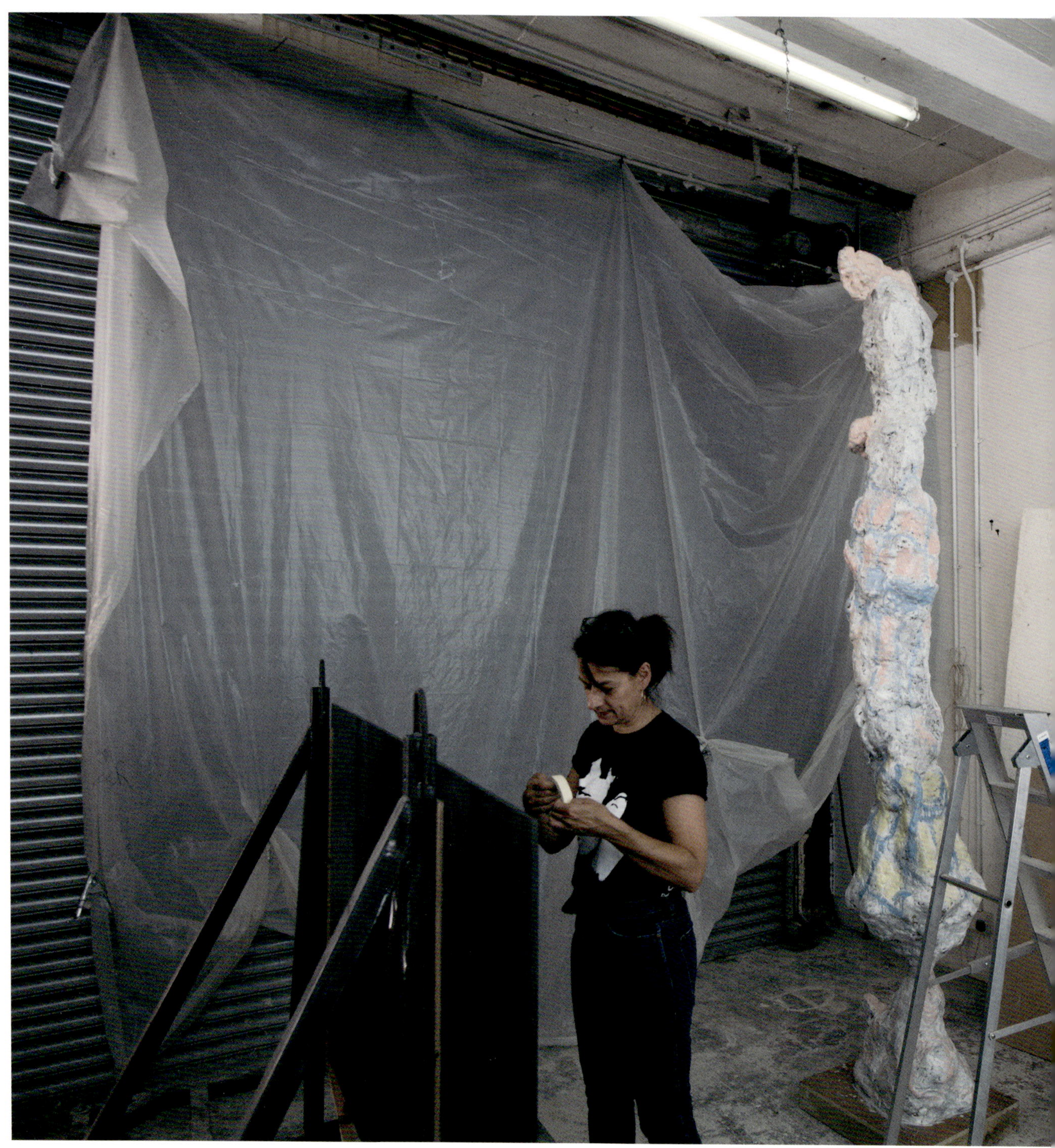

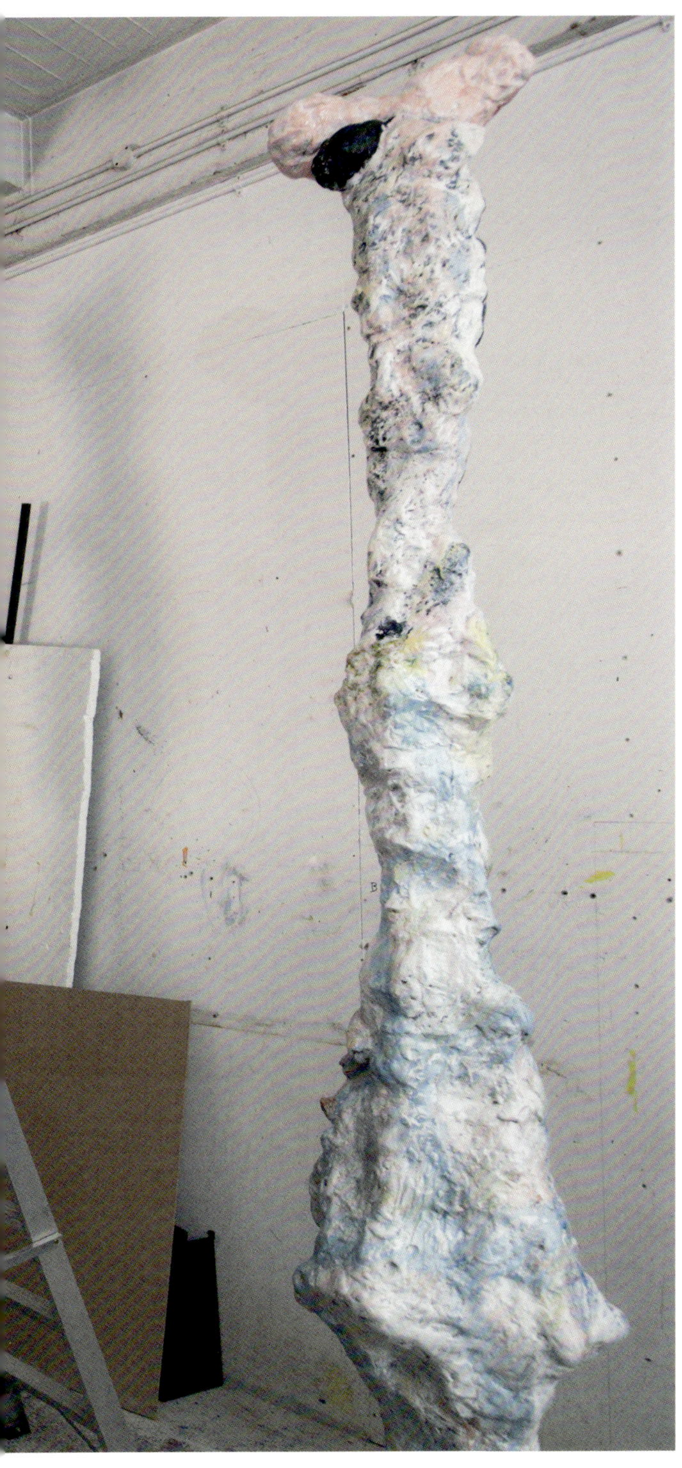

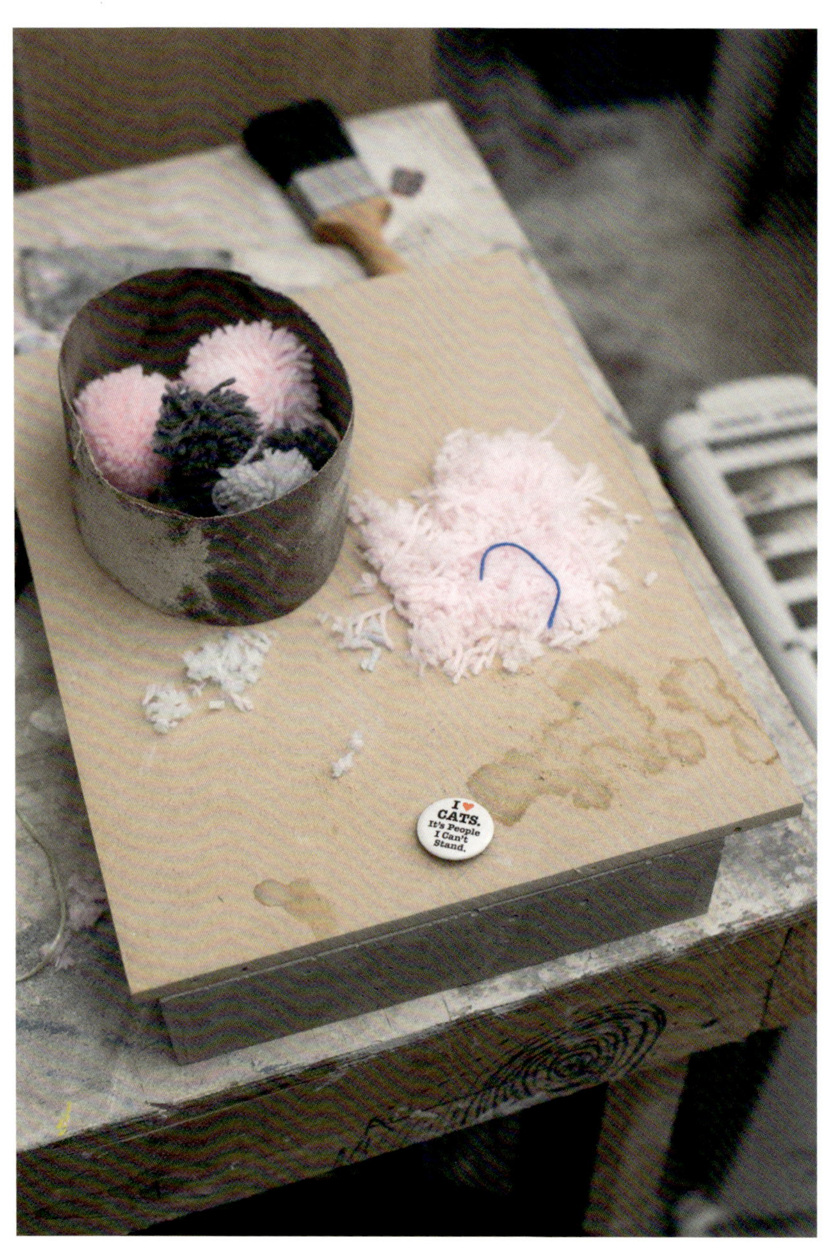
I ♥ CATS.
It's People
I Can't
Stand.

It feels important that this is the inaugural exhibition at Tate St Ives' new gallery space. As we move into a new era of programming with this expansion, for the first time Tate St Ives is able to permanently display the collection alongside an ambitious temporary exhibitions programme. St Ives, which has long been a site for radical artistic practice, experimentation and the international exchange of ideas, is a fitting host for this exhibition by an artist whose work has consistently challenged convention.

Rebecca Warren (born 1965) first came to prominence in the 1990s and became known internationally for her exuberant, roughly worked clay sculptures, bronzes and steel constructions, which engage with the history of sculpture and her position within this tradition. Drawing on a myriad of sources including art history, film, pop culture and music, this powerful body of new or previously unseen work is the artist's first solo exhibition in the UK in eight years.

Rebecca Warren: All That Heaven Allows presents sculptures, assemblages and constructions in a variety of materials including clay, bronze, steel and neon. In her approach to material, surface and scale, Warren pushes the boundaries of sculpture in a way that is decidedly her own. From the weighty to the delicate, the serious to the playful – or an unexpected combination of both – her work navigates through multiple artistic traditions, often with varied measures of irreverent or appreciative attention to the work of her predominately male precursors. Warren's placement of sculptures in space is deliberate and considered, allowing each work to possess its own energy while being in active and conscious relation to one another. The resulting groupings and sightlines in this exhibition create different associations and resonances, offering an ever-shifting set of experiences.

Thanks are due to all the staff at Tate St Ives who have worked on this exhibition and publication, in particular Exhibitions and Displays Curator, Laura Smith, as well as our colleagues in Tate Conservation and Registration. We would also like to thank all those who have helped make this exhibition possible, including Maureen Paley, Max Hetzler, Matthew Marks and their teams, as well as The Rebecca Warren Exhibition Supporters Group, Tate Members and Tate St Ives Members. Thanks also to Damon Murray and Stephen Sorrell at FUEL for designing this beautiful publication, to Andrew Miller for his help and support, and of course, our biggest thanks to Rebecca for her dedication, ideas and extraordinary work.

REBECCA WARREN

IN CONVER SATION

LAURA SMITH

LS: Given the varied nature of your work, I would like to start at the beginning.
How does your work begin?

RW: I don't really know where it comes from. From a sort of strange nowhere.
Then gradually something comes out into the light. There are impulses, half-
seen shapes, things that might have stuck with you from decades ago, as well
as more recently. It's all stuff in the world going through you as a filter...

That's interesting, that semi-conscious drive – how does it relate to the work
you are making for St Ives?

My attitude here has largely been to make new work for what is a new venue.
Although all the individual works stand on their own, I'm also always conscious
of arranging a specific show, thinking about the scale and feel of the venue,
how people will move in it, how the work hangs together, what happens as it's
travelled through... Since this particular space is brand new, it's a bit more of a
tall order to know the space and what it needs and what can work in there.
And then there's the special and peculiar thing about St Ives and its history. St
Ives is at the edge of the land, so it's like a sort of concentrated sump of all
sorts of things – gentility, excellence, bland strangeness – a lot of things. There's
something very pagan in there too.

Could you talk a little about your references and how broad-ranging they are?
I mean, when I look at your work I am thinking about Willem de Kooning and
Minnie Mouse simultaneously, or about Alberto Giacometti and The Michael
Zager Band (whose 1977 disco hit *Let's All Chant* you've used as the title for
one of your recent sculptures). How do these things come together?

Things of any kind come up from below, much more than they are dropped
from above by me. That's how they have to work otherwise they're add-ons,
dubious justifications... You discover what bits of the world keep nagging at you
and fascinating you because they won't leave you or your work alone. In my
case, there are lots of things including artists' works from the fairly distant and
recent past – Rodin, Picasso, de Kooning, etc. And there have been Helmut
Newton's photographs and Robert Crumb's cartoons... and a whole lot of other
stuff – the New York Dolls, Bowie... The Michael Zager Band's *Let's All Chant*
probably surfaced because of its insane glam – overcooked to an unusual
degree: '*Your body, my body, everybody move your body...*'

Yes! And these things often also find their way into your studio, physically –
from a picture of an enraged Maria Callas to a photograph of a cat by Peter
Fischli and David Weiss that was made into the cover of *Parkett* magazine, and
which you labelled with a post-it note reading 'NO!'... What's the importance of
surrounding yourself with certain images or objects in the place where you work?

I collect pictures and notes that have some potential, or are funny, or help rather
than hinder. The studio is where the mess coagulates into certain kinds of
realities. Nothing else happens in there – which makes a studio quite a strange
place in the general run of the world, like a slightly crazy shrine to your own
thought processes. The *Parkett* cover was a turning point for me because when
I first saw it I realised that art could be a picture of a cat standing on a rainy
pavement. I realised that I didn't have to fear things that I liked. I didn't need
permission to like them. I had to unlearn the 80s Goldsmiths (where I did my
BA) ethos where we were supposed to believe in a certain kind of conceptualism
that proved itself to be detrimental to creative thinking and action. I would
never put pictures on my studio walls in case they were wrong! When I met artist
Fergal Stapleton (during my MA at Chelsea) he told me that I could start with
the material itself, and begin my relationship to some kind of inchoate idea or
impulse in that way. I could choose a material, and the art would tell me what
it might be as it developed in that material. This was a crucial breakthrough...
The 'NO!' post-it note came later when I knew I had to stop looking at it and
get on with my own work. The same was true when I super-glued the pages of
my Martin Kippenberger book together.

Could you say something more about your relationship to the materials you use
– clay, bronze, steel, pompoms, paper, neon. What is your attraction to each
material and how do they relate to one another?

I have always varied materials in order to keep things open, and not get stuck.
Sometimes I use paper in collages and constructions. I like impermanence, lightness.
There's also an element of early learning when using paper – of scribbling,
tearing, discarding. It's nice to bring those things to the centre sometimes.
I first used neon in collaboration with Fergal Stapleton in the early 90s. We
didn't want to use it in a way that stuck too closely to its normal use – making
words, declarative phrases (as those who immediately followed us – into the
exact same neon shop! – did). We liked its other qualities, as a material, an
element in a field. I still use it like this. At first I couldn't afford it so I would use

bits they threw out, which for some reason was mainly the letter O. So a lot of my early vitrines had Os in them. Neon glows and spreads the colour. Where that colour ends is hard to define. That's a thing I like. I often paint the neon glass, or half-obscure it with other elements in a collage or a vitrine. It's a strange material, half-seen even when you look straight at it. Its nature is incidental, mystical light.

Steel has its unshakeable macho connotations – but that's not all it's got. I like to paint it sometimes, to mess about with it, to put a pompom or some other little element on it. It's a ground and it's the thing itself. It's heavy and dark and in the way and very present – like a bad shadow.

You can polish nice highlights into bronze. If you paint it, it becomes made of paint throughout – or the paint has form – or the two impact each other at odd mental angles.

Some of my work is made to be cast in bronze, some is made to stay as clay. I first used clay in 1998 with *Helmut Crumb* followed by my show *The Agony and the Ecstasy* at Maureen Paley in 2000, which predominantly consisted of clay works. Using clay was extremely unfashionable at that time. People laughed at me and thought I'd lost my mind. But I knew I had found something quite powerful and real for me.

Pompoms are so gorgeous, why *wouldn't* you have them in your art?! Put onto other materials, they destabilise the inherent qualities. They reduce weight. They float, they land. They're like dustballs. They're decorative and intrinsic at the same time. When you put any of these things together, if you follow some need in these relationships, they can go off into strange places...

And how do these materials change the way you work? You've spoken in the past about pushing and pulling and manipulating clay, which you then solidify – along with your own fingerprints – in bronze, as opposed to the less conscious and more chance circumstances in which the collages are made?

It's all manipulation. The human hand can do a lot of things. Exact levels of consciousness and chance are indefinable. There's always a tension between doing and being done to – or channelling. It's all one, since even the most deliberate act is made from the dark unknown stuff beneath the surface of your mind.

So is there is an autobiographical aspect to your work?

I don't think it can be otherwise. It's all happening in the machine of your head, the person, the mess of experience. You can't make someone else's art. It is

surprising how you can be reminded that you were always going to end up
doing this stuff anyway. My mum showed me all these drawings I did as a kid of
twin ballerinas standing on a box. I had forgotten about them, but there they
are in my grown-up art: doubled ballerinas on their shared plinth. Strange!

For me, there are also always allusions to various cultural (both high and low)
clichés of femininity in your work, which you twist and distort in ways that are
pointed, or funny, or exaggerated, or heart-breaking. I wonder if you could
describe what these allusions do for you? I understand your position as much
more complex than just thinking about a re-appropriation of the female form,
and more about how culture and history serve artists working today, or perpetuate
certain expectations.

I like to mix things up, turn things on their heads. I'm not a stickler for thinking
there is, or isn't, a categorical difference between high and low, so I mess
around in there too. In the end, you like the things you like, and if you like the
whole of something, that's noticeable. I like the whole of Rodin and Iggy Pop,
for instance, and almost the whole of the Todds (Solondz and Haynes, film
directors)... When I was drawn to clay, I was also drawn to Crumb and his way
of getting to his own desirable forms without worrying about disapproval.
Cartoons boil everything down to essential curves. It was a useful – and risky –
place to start when I was trying to get an understanding of my own ideas. I
used to worry a lot about meaning and where it should come from. Initially I
wanted my work to be robustly female, to push that side of things, and this
helped in that it allowed me to make anything at all! Starting out, I was holding
on to the idea that I needed these anchors to make things. That's pretty much
cured now and I've gone on without any need for these qualifiers. Ultimately, I
realised that my brain just doesn't work like that. I gradually discovered that,
for me, art is made from freedom and openness to possibilities. Hopefully the
realities in all this and the actual answers to these questions emerge in precise
forms in the art that I make.

This is also interesting in terms of the way you title your works and exhibitions,
which calls to mind many of those high and/or low references to films and
songs and other artists – sometimes explicitly, sometimes more obscurely. How
do your titles come to be?

Words and phrases float about and get caught… sometimes way in advance of a work or an exhibition. Sometimes the title is waiting for the art, sometimes it's the other way around. In any case, we're talking about something's name. The right name. That's the thing. Often I'm looking at a particular work of mine, asking the question: *What is your name?*

So, how do you think all of these ideas will emerge in what you are making for Tate St Ives?

For St Ives, I've revisited *Let's All Chant* 2017 which is a large, pink steel work. It seemed like it could have another life in another venue. (The earlier version was shown at Matthew Marks Gallery in LA.) I've made five new large bronze sculptures. They're recognisably from a certain family of my work, but there's always some new form or idea at play. They seem quite pagan, like standing stones. Putting them on the floor without plinths will make them very present in a different way. I've also revisited *Los Hadeans* 2017 (from the same show in LA), another series of bronze sculptures – painting them differently – and this will be the first time anything from this family has been seen in the UK. There are also collages I made a while ago and have never shown till now. It occurred to me that these works are only realised fully once they're shown. Till then they're full of a kind of latency – latency peculiar to themselves. I wanted to resist just making giant things for a big room. Everything is always made at its finished size, never scaled up from maquettes. Always hand-eye, hand-eye.

One thing that I am very excited about in your St Ives exhibition is the space that you have given to your works, and the shifts in rhythm and pace that you have created between them. How did you go about planning the installation – especially for a space that hadn't been built yet?

I was keen to keep the gallery as a vast, concrete subterranean space lit by huge skylights. I wanted newness for a new space, and I wanted people to see the space before it gets divided and partitioned for future exhibitions. Giant spaces tend to make people want to look at the whole thing from the doorway! So I wanted to interrupt the entrance to a certain extent, to encourage them to move around the space in a particular way in order to fully discover the work. Some way into the process of planning an exhibition, I use scale models of the space and the works. Between the model and the reality, there's a third interesting version. I think of the space, and the show in it, like one of my own vitrines in which I arrange various found and made elements. Or like Giacometti's sculpture, *The Palace at 4 a.m.*

Apart from the scale of the new gallery in St Ives, how has the location and history of the town affected your decisions when making and thinking about the exhibition?

> I went there to see how it is, to try and pick up something from it – St Ives' history, the ghost of Hepworth. It was nice to look again at Hepworth. A continuity of that history is always in play in circumstances as dense as these: here were the post-war modernists, the post-Picassoists, working out and enjoying new possibilities. We're post that, two and three generations later. Each generation has more to go on – or more to ignore. Once I had sort of taken in St Ives, I tried to forget it… I wanted to avoid pastiche and generalisation. St Ives is quite a mad place in a way. It's the end of the world, the bottom of the Earth, down and down. The title for the exhibition came to me quite early on – *All That Heaven Allows*. Optimism and limitation. No matter what, this is as far as you can go.

Finally, you once said that it takes quite a lot of balls to stand in front of one of your sculptures and say, 'I made that.' Could you tell me what you meant by that, and do you still feel the same way?

> You make the art you make, not the art you think you should make, or the art you wish you could make… There is a point when you have to accept what it is that you actually can do. I think I'm a bit out there on my own with the things I make. I think my level of commitment to the actual demands of the art itself, the forms themselves, is unusual. It can run away with you and you have to accept it. It can take you by surprise and not be the thing you expected. In the early days my sculptures weren't crated – just wheeled out to the lorries. So there'd be blokey shippers pushing the sculptures by their curvy extremities: many opportunities to be mortified!
>
> It's all made from what you take in. And you have to make it all from a good unconscious place, not your ego. I have followed the art where it leads. Something in the various scales and general appearances can be quite awkward and so quite worrisome to stand next to and boldly claim them as your own. After all, this is me. This is my mind, my life. They are exposures of my intimate relations to art and the world.

REBECCA WARREN

ALL THAT HEAVEN ALLOWS

LAURA SMITH

I, too, overflow; my desires have invented new desires, my body knows unheard-of songs. Time and again I, too, have felt so full of luminous torrents that I could burst – burst with forms much more beautiful than those which are put up in frames and sold for a fortune. And I, too, said nothing, showed nothing; I didn't open my mouth, I didn't repaint my half of the world. I was ashamed. I was afraid, and I swallowed my shame and my fear. I said to myself: You are mad! What's the meaning of these waves, these floods, these outbursts? Where is the ebullient infinite woman who ... hasn't been ashamed of her strength? Who, surprised and horrified by the fantastic tumult of her drives (for she was made to believe that a well-adjusted normal woman has a ... divine composure), hasn't accused herself of being a monster? Who, feeling a funny desire stirring inside her (to sing, to write, to dare to speak, in short, to bring out something new), hasn't thought she was sick? Well, her shameful sickness is that she resists death, that she makes trouble.[i]

All That Heaven Allows is a 1955 Technicolor romance directed by Douglas Sirk, starring Jane Wyman and Rock Hudson. It follows a blossoming love affair between an upper-class American widow (Cary) and her handsome, younger gardener (Ron). When their relationship prompts the disdain of her country club friends, Cary is forced to make the difficult choice between love and the approval of her community. In 2002, Todd Haynes' film *Far From Heaven* paid homage to *All That Heaven Allows*, telling the story of Cathy Whitaker (played by Julianne Moore), a 1950s housewife living in wealthy suburban Connecticut, who falls scandalously in love with her younger, African-American gardener, Raymond (played by Dennis Haysbert).

By using the title *All That Heaven Allows* for her exhibition, Rebecca Warren calls to mind the content and construction of the two films, both of which are beautifully crafted and full of texture, light and colour play, as well as a sort of hysterical intensity which carries the expectations placed on Cary and Cathy – towards beauty, conformity and perfection – through the films. Both women seethe with urges that don't fit the cultural and societal roles assigned to them, raising questions about how a woman in 1950s American suburbia was expected to behave, look and fall in love. With Warren, this thinking might extend to what a woman artist is expected to make, or who she might be expected to cite as her influences. However, these are limitations that she certainly doesn't suffer from. Warren's endeavour is to make art that is entirely without gendered justifications – to make what she wants without excuses, complaints or qualifiers. This is her power. Any parameters that she may encounter do not come from societal expectations but from something far less conscious or recognisable, from somewhere within art itself. As she states: 'the need persists to follow each artistic endeavour as far as you can, in the knowledge that there is an upper limit to the amount that we can ever see or know, but within which we can still experience art as an infinitely strange and elusive enterprise.'[ii]

Warren's clay, bronze and steel sculptures alike are often large, bold, (deliberately) ungainly and self-assured. They employ – sometimes overtly, sometimes obliquely

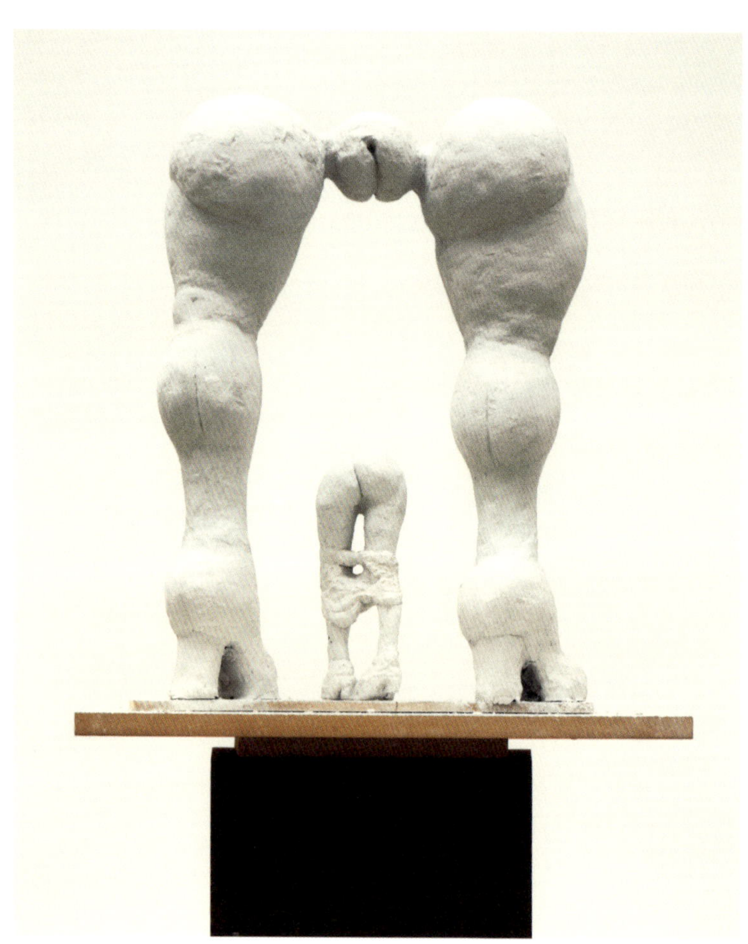

Helmut Crumb
1998
Clay on MDF on painted MDF plinths
55.9 x 50.8 x 38.1 cm

– a vernacular of art historical references, many of which are perhaps not what a woman artist might be expected to invoke. Alongside her allusions to popular culture, which come through titles shared with pop songs and films, or imagery that sometimes verges on the cartoonish or Disney-esque, Warren also calls forth the ghosts of artists such as Willem de Kooning, Edgar Degas, Alberto Giacometti, Jean-Honoré Fragonard, Auguste Rodin, Umberto Boccioni, and others. And yet she consistently, consciously and playfully counters the collective weight of these artists and their art historical genealogies through the skirts, cartoon bows, Minnie-Mouse shoes, boobs, bottoms, and bulges of her sculptures. That said, her work is not simply a militant re-appropriation of womanhood. It is a much more complex and interesting undertaking. It is the gathering of forces, and the crystallisation of countless influences into unique and strange forms, which, in their making, become far more than the sum of their parts.

And there is pleasure in the making of these strange forms. Taking joy from her various materials and the varying qualities they possess, Warren's works explore materiality alongside these ideas of precedence, purpose and tradition. In an interview with Julia Peyton-Jones and Hans Ulrich Obrist, Warren outlines how, a few years after graduating from art school, she allowed herself to look back at the history which she had shut out because it wasn't accepted at Goldsmiths – and she was able to let it into her work: 'I was trying to occupy the space of the work of those male artists and see what that told me.'iii In this way, it could be imagined that all of Warren's work is to some extent autobiographical, or a way of examining her relationship to these histories and ideas. Through her satirical and discordant allusions to art history, popular culture and the female form, Warren 'makes tangible her struggle with process and precedence; with irregularity and exploration; with looking and looking again, and then changing your mind just when you think you've got it'.iv

Early works such as *Helmut Crumb* 1998 and *Croccioni* 2000 can be seen as pivotal moments in the evolution of Warren's career. These pieces demonstrate her burgeoning, humorous way of looking at, while participating in, a lineage of art historical standards – a position which she describes as always 'deliberately precarious'.v *Helmut Crumb* consists of two pairs of women's legs made from raw clay. Each grounded by a pair of high-heeled shoes, there is something simultaneously ancient and cartoonish about them. One pair, the larger of the two, has a wide stance and seems almost to be a gateway or portal. The crotch appears as a solid, clefted sphere of clay – a tennis ball, perhaps – almost separate from the thighs on either side of it, so that it seems on the verge of becoming an independent object, a force in its own right. The second pair is much smaller and more fragile, her legs more coquettish as she appears to lean forward, her pants nearly at her ankles. The style of this second pair is realistic and naturalistic, more the stuff of life modelling. It stands under the portal of the other legs, sheltered and framed by it. Arranged like this, there is the definite possibility that one could be the offspring of the other – or, at any rate, that a lineage of some kind is being presented. The first, large pair of legs is taken from a drawing, *Girls, Girls, Girls* 1972 by 1970s counterculture cartoonist

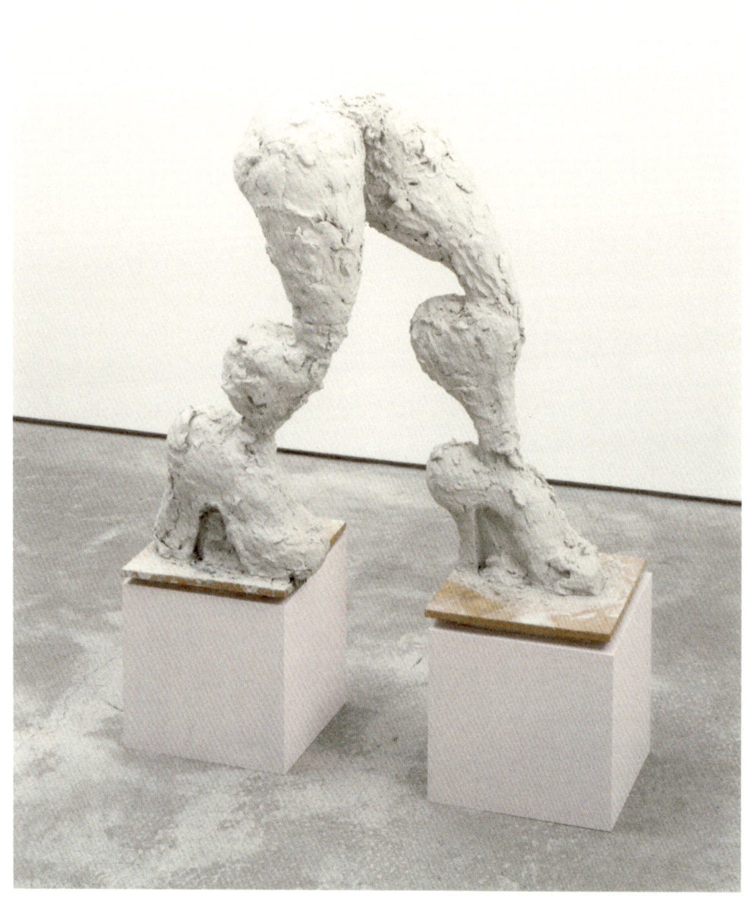

Croccioni
2000
Clay on MDF on painted MDF plinths
85 x 34 x 84 cm

Robert Crumb, which depicts a woman whose shape keeps changing until she ends up as a disembodied pair of legs – or, as Warren has said, 'like a monumental piece of architecture'.[vi] The second pair is from a photograph by the German fashion photographer Helmut Newton. Taken from the book *White Women* 1976, Warren has said of these photographs that they make the women look like 'homunculi, shrunken in scale to fit the pages'.[vii] *Croccioni* contains another pair of Crumb-like, raw clay women's legs – curvy, almost modular, like stacked commas or cartoonish hams. This time they straddle two plinths as though striding forward, reminiscent of the album cover for Rod Stewart's *Atlantic Crossing* 1975, or a late take on Umberto Boccioni's *Unique Forms of Continuity in Space* 1913.

There is an evident mix of joy and discomfort in the over-determined sexuality of much of Warren's work, which charts her admiration for her artistic forerunners and the extent to which she allows herself to be influenced by them, as well as challenge them. As Gregorio Magnani has stated: the works are 'enjoying their status as objects of the gaze and are ready to kick open the door and reveal Degas' embarrassing erection.'[viii] Her works are indecent and intimate, formal and grotesque. They show figures in flux – metamorphosing in and out of their material and distorting our ability to recognise and hold on to images. They have a mutating quality – twisting, turning, sensual and urgent – and yet remain wholly self-possessed and poised. There is no quick fix or easy translation of meaning in all this. The component parts, antecedents and formative impulses of Warren's works are hard to pick apart, and hard to unravel – and so they ultimately require us to examine our own perceptions. As Barry Schwabsky explains: 'you're not just meant to get a certain feeling from the work; you're meant to examine the feelings you have about having those feelings.'[ix]

Nearly twenty years on, Warren's new works provide a posterior re-assessment of her earlier pieces. In the wake of the works they precede, *Helmut Crumb* and *Croccioni* can now be seen as so much more than witty collisions of references to other artists: they are complex, fierce and satirical calling cards. The new works have become more nuanced, more knowing and more self-assured. They have matured, asserting their own identities to become forms as free of their parentage as anything or anyone reasonably can be. That is not to say that the new sculptures are no longer bold or gallant or playful. Works such as *The Three* 2017, sculpted in clay, cast in bronze, then hand-painted in loose strokes of pastel or metallic paint, maintain the visual memories from art history plus the fleshy lumps and sensual bulges of Warren's older works – just now made all the more weighty (excuse the pun) by the symbolic heaviness of their material make-up. And bronze, too, provides their silhouettes of overhangs and swellings, and their totem-like height, a robustness that clay just couldn't manage.

The new smaller bronzes are slender and lumpen, like 'stalagmites built not from minerals and salt, but from a plethora of archetypes, clichés and inventions'.[x] Titled *Los Hadeans* 2017, they make reference to the Greek term Hades – once a god and later a place: the Greek underworld. Like proto-beings rising from

the heat and darkness, these figures appear variously confident or nonchalant in their body language as they stand hands-on-hips, cross-legged or matador-like, lightly painted with small strokes, traces of tartan, glyphs, and strange symbols, and finished occasionally with a single pompom. Warren's frequent use of a bow or pompom could be seen as a tongue-in-cheek celebration of her position in the history of sculpture. But these materials also perform a range of subtler functions – a dalliance with formalism, a sort of provocative interruption of sculptural traditions. Used to disrupt the surface of her works, the pompoms also *become* the surface of her works, transformed into pigment and shape, bringing everything in and around them into a new dimension.

The pompoms also feature in many of Warren's steel works. These sheet metal constructions may initially feel at odds with the organic exuberance of her bronze and clay sculptures, but they nonetheless follow a similar impulse to both tease and participate in the lineage of art historical standards. The larger steel sculptures are tectonic and architectural. They evoke the traditions of constructivist and minimalist sculpture, though some also lean towards the figurative or resemble intimate and domestic items, such as the bed-like *Let's All Chant* 2017, which takes its title from The Michael Zager Band's 1977 disco hit. Often their forms seem precariously balanced, as though they might topple over at any point, yet they are held together (almost magnetically) by some invisible force or magical centre of gravity. Warren sometimes treats the surfaces of these works in the same way as her clay and bronze figures – with touches of paint – but more often they are left as raw steel, or powder coated with one solid colour – a sort of dirty baby pink – and then finished with a final pompom.

And the pompoms make a regular appearance in Warren's collages and works with neon too. These are perhaps the most intimate of her works, both because of their scale and because of the items that they are made from: detritus, strands of wool, hair, fluff, clay, and pieces of coloured neon tubing – some of which are bent and twisted to match the contours of her own face. These collages show us an atomised, miniature version of her world. When making them, Warren says that she is trying to get something truthful to happen – 'the process is that strange mix of doing and happening'[xi] – and the results could be seen as a series of intimate self-portraits of Warren and her studio.

A large proportion of Warren's works bear vestiges of her. The haptic surfaces of her clay and bronze works trace the lines of her touch, her fingerprints and her palm. They wear the marks of her making – massaged, squeezed and pushed: 'My hands are big! … They follow the winding paths of my thoughts. They imitate visions. I am a mime artist.'[xii] These works are generous in their materiality, establishing themselves within history, popular culture, tradition and a pleasure in what can be made with inert materials. They are alloys of rudimentary form and contradictory information, engendering corporeal and cerebral sensations simultaneously. As she comments: 'my sculptures often come out of a bucket of clay, and they only get as far from there as they need to in order to convincingly claim freedom and separation from that bucket.'[xiii]

In all of Warren's works, not just the clay and bronze pieces, meanings amalgamate, ossify, break down, re-circulate and multiply. It is as though she is performing a standoff between resolution and irresolution, minimalism and maximalism. Our reactions can be both analytic and physical, rational and irrational. For these reasons, the ways in which the works are presented and displayed are vital to Warren. Their placement is paced and measured so that the rhythm of their encounter and the meter of their polymorphous voices can be carefully choreographed. In St Ives, with its strong history of paganism, folklore and the occult, the particular arrangement of works in *All That Heaven Allows* could be reminiscent of standing stones, magic circles and ley lines of ancient significance – groupings which 'reinforce the works' elemental attributes and the strange transformation of matter into meanings.'[xiv] But the magic of Warren's exhibition lies not in a direct allusion to these spiritual formations, but in the close attention that has been given to the conditions and energy of each sculpture. There is a tension, delicacy and intimacy to the way in which Warren approaches the arrangement of her works in space, one that mirrors her approach to history (whether that be of materials, art, or popular culture) and which kindles a shifting atmosphere of empathy, elusivity of meaning, desire and embarrassment in and around the works: a kind of conjury that holds the works together but also lets them mutate and change organically as we move around them. As Warren says: 'maybe there's a kind of alchemy in this no-man's land, where the base state is movement and transformation.'[xv]

Warren's works, from clay to bronze to steel to paper to neon to pompom, may be all that heaven allows, and that is no bad thing. The magic of their making and exhibition is, in turn, that our encounter with them can be whatever heaven allows us to grasp.

i Hélène Cixous, 'The Laugh of the Medusa', 1975, trans. by Keith Cohen and Paula Cohen, *Signs*, vol.1, no.4, Summer 1976, p.876.
ii Rebecca Warren, conversation with the author, summer 2017.
iii Rebecca Warren, interview with Julia Peyton-Jones and Hans Ulrich Obrist, in *Rebecca Warren*, exh. cat., Serpentine Gallery, London, March–April 2009, p.64.
iv Jennifer Higgie, 'Under the Influence: Rebecca Warren', *Frieze*, no.72, January–February 2003, p.67
v Rebecca Warren, conversation with the author, summer 2017.
vi Rebecca Warren, interview with Carl Freedman, in *Rebecca Warren*, exh. cat., Kunsthalle Zürich, April–May 2004, p.20.
vii Ibid.
viii Gregorio Magnani, 'Dark Passage', in Kunsthalle Zürich 2004, p.50.
ix Barry Schwabsky, 'Fragments', in Serpentine Gallery 2009, p.43.
x Jörg Heiser, 'Bronze Heads and Hair Bows', in *Rebecca Warren*, exh. cat., Galerie Max Hetzler, Berlin, April–June 2012, p.5.
xi Rebecca Warren, conversation with the author, summer 2017.
xii Rebecca Warren, in conversation with Albert Oehlen, 'Material Object', *Mousse*, no.53, April–May 2016, p.143.
xiii Ibid., p.142.
xiv Rebecca Warren, conversation with the author, summer 2017.
xv Rebecca Warren, interview with Julia Peyton-Jones and Hans Ulrich Obrist, in Serpentine Gallery 2009, p.66.

LIST OF WORKS

There's No Other Way
2010–17
Hand-painted bronze
300 x 69 x 71 cm

The Three
2017
Hand-painted bronze
292 x 51 x 46 cm

Jean
2017
Hand-painted bronze
269 x 61 x 55 cm

Rainer
2017
Hand-painted bronze
299 x 51 x 46 cm

Aurelius
2017
Hand-painted bronze
295 x 58 x 49 cm

These Patriarchs
2017
Clay, twig and pompom
on MDF on wheels
194 x 89 x 100 cm

Los Hadeans (I)
2017
Hand-painted bronze on
painted MDF plinth
bronze: 160 x 61 x 25 cm
plinth: 25 x 75 x 60 cm

Los Hadeans (III)
2017
Hand-painted bronze
and pompom on
painted MDF plinth
bronze: 212 x 103 x 30 cm
plinth: 17 x 106 x 68 cm

Los Hadeans (V)
2017
Hand-painted bronze on
painted MDF plinth
bronze: 126 x 17 x 14 cm
plinth: 36 x 33 x 32 cm

Los Hadeans (VI)
2017
Hand-painted bronze on
painted MDF plinth
bronze: 127 x 52 x 23 cm
plinth: 25 x 55 x 40 cm

Los Hadeans (VII)
2017
Hand-painted bronze on
painted MDF plinth
bronze: 120 x 30 x 18 cm
plinth: 25 x 33 x 33 cm

Collage
2003
Mixed media on MDF
40 x 60 x 7 cm

Collage
2003
Mixed media on MDF
62 x 44 x 7 cm

Ulrike
2003
Mixed media on MDF
62 x 45 x 7 cm

Homo Sapiens
2005
Mixed media on MDF
60 x 63 x 8 cm

The Cat Stays in the Picture
2010
Mixed media on MDF
81 x 61 x 12.5 cm

*Manliness without
ostentation (I learnt from
what I heard and can
remember of my father)*
2017
Mixed media on MDF
56 x 33 x 9 cm

Shollage
2017
Mixed media on MDF
49.5 x 30 x 11 cm

Old Age 2
2017
Mixed media on MDF
56.5 x 119.5 x 15 cm

Child of Nature
2017
Mixed media on MDF
122 x 89 x 13 cm

The Sea
2017
Hand-painted steel
and pompom on
painted MDF plinth
steel: 115 x 230 x 119 cm
plinth: 20 x 295 x 180 cm

Let's All Chant (reprise)
2017
Painted steel and pompom
139 x 269 x 396 cm

All that Heaven Allows
2017
Mixed media on MDF
52 x 31 x 8 cm

Telepathy
2017
Hand-painted steel
266 x 113 x 23 cm

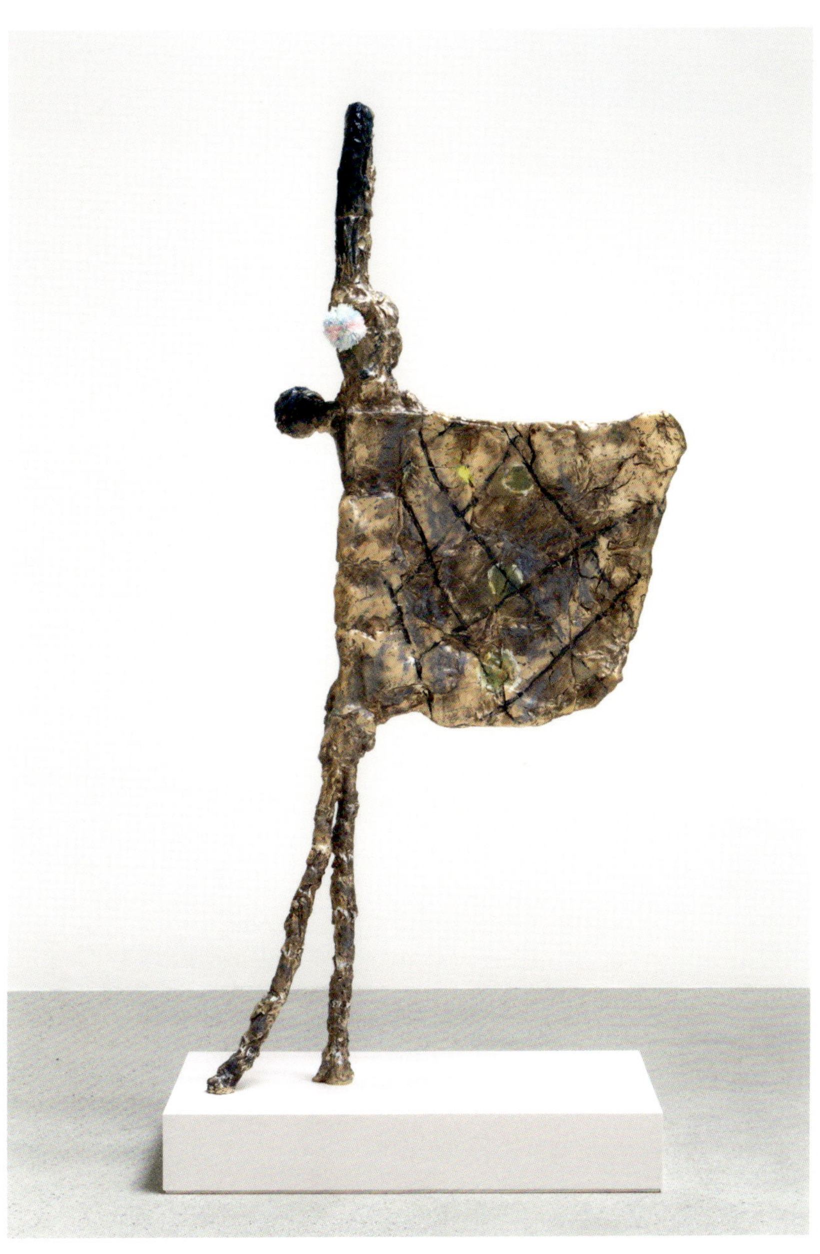

Los Hadeans (III)
2017

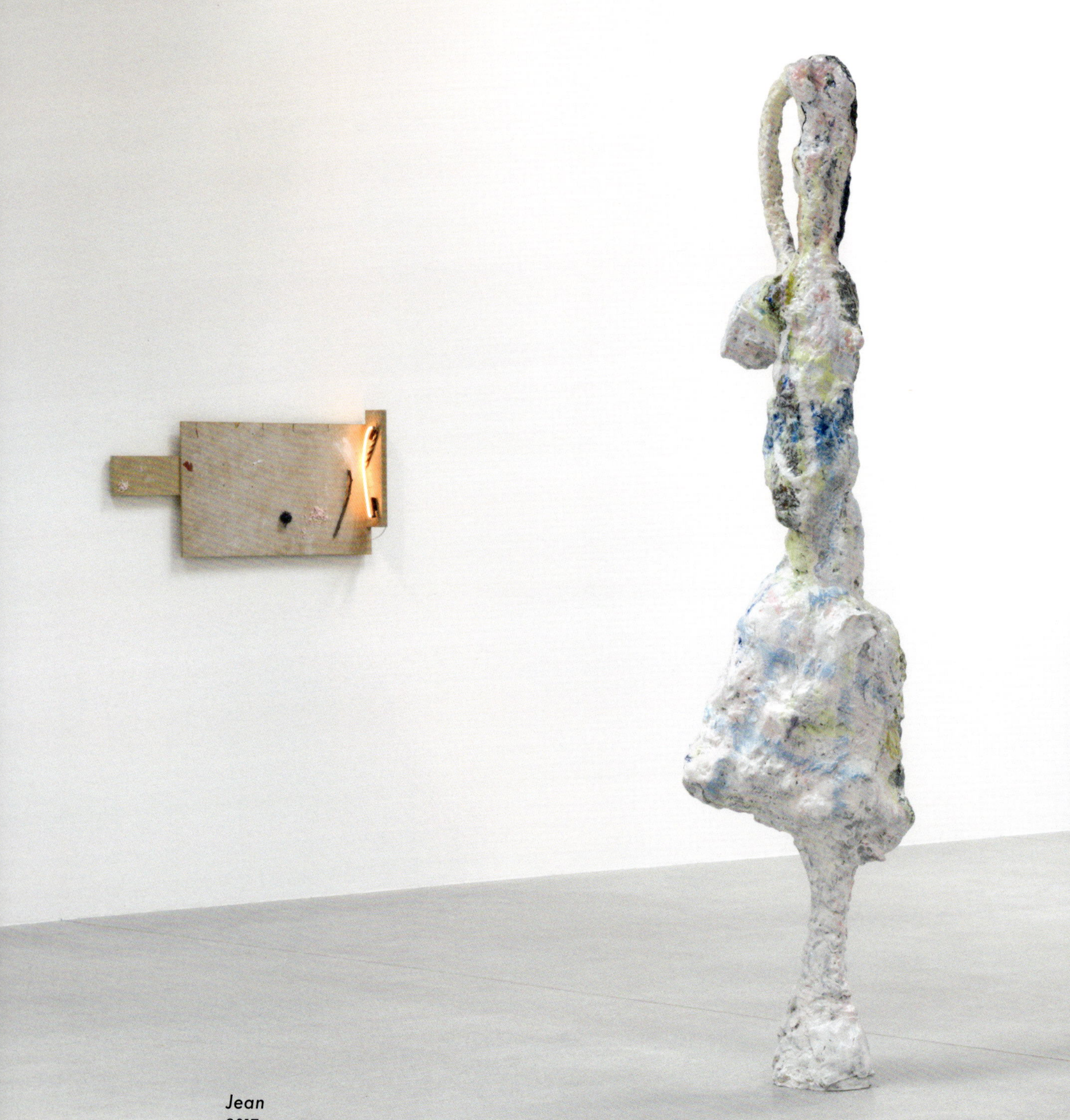

Jean
2017

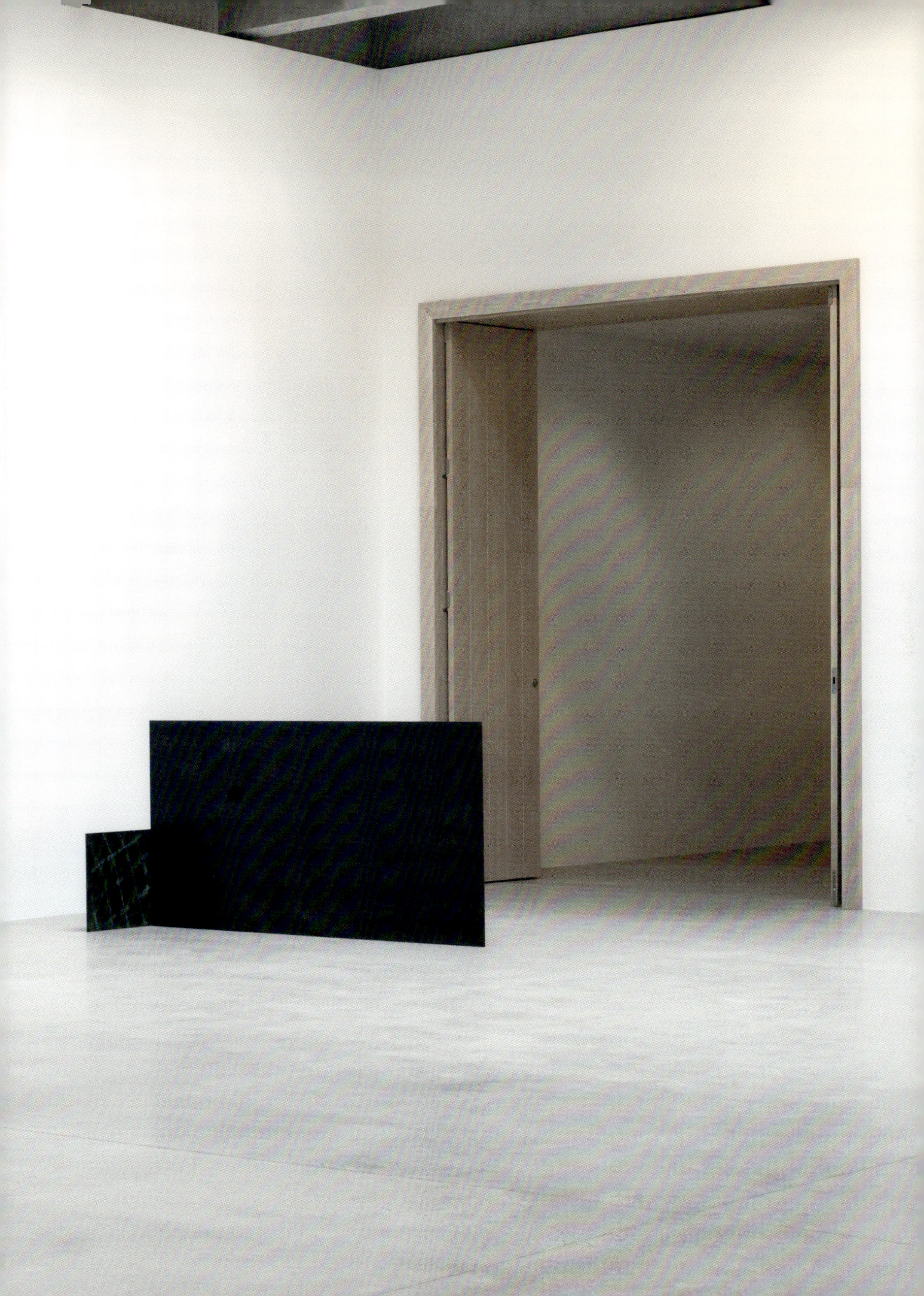

Old Age 2
2017

The Sea
2017

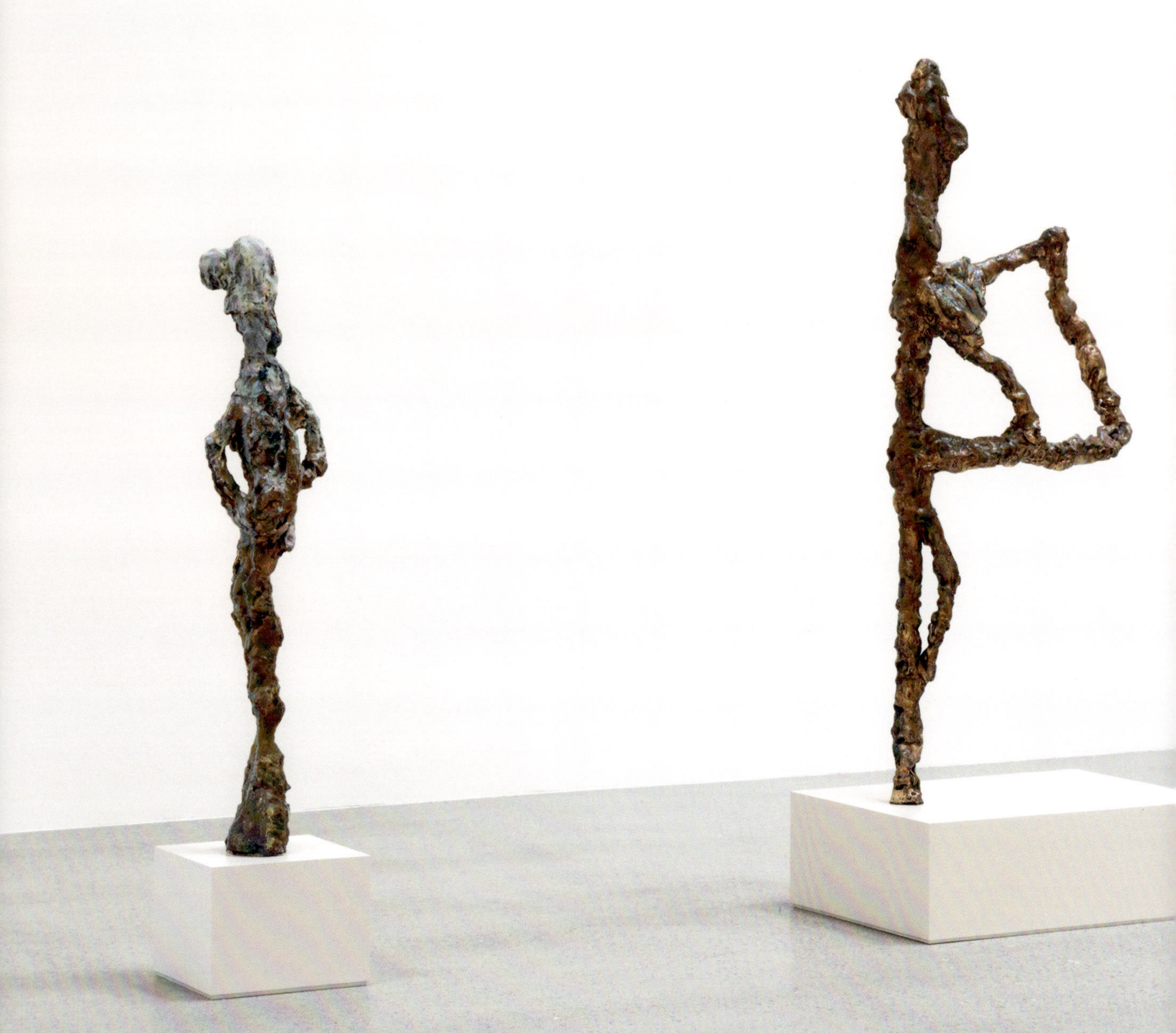

Los Hadeans (VII), (I), (V), (VI)
2017

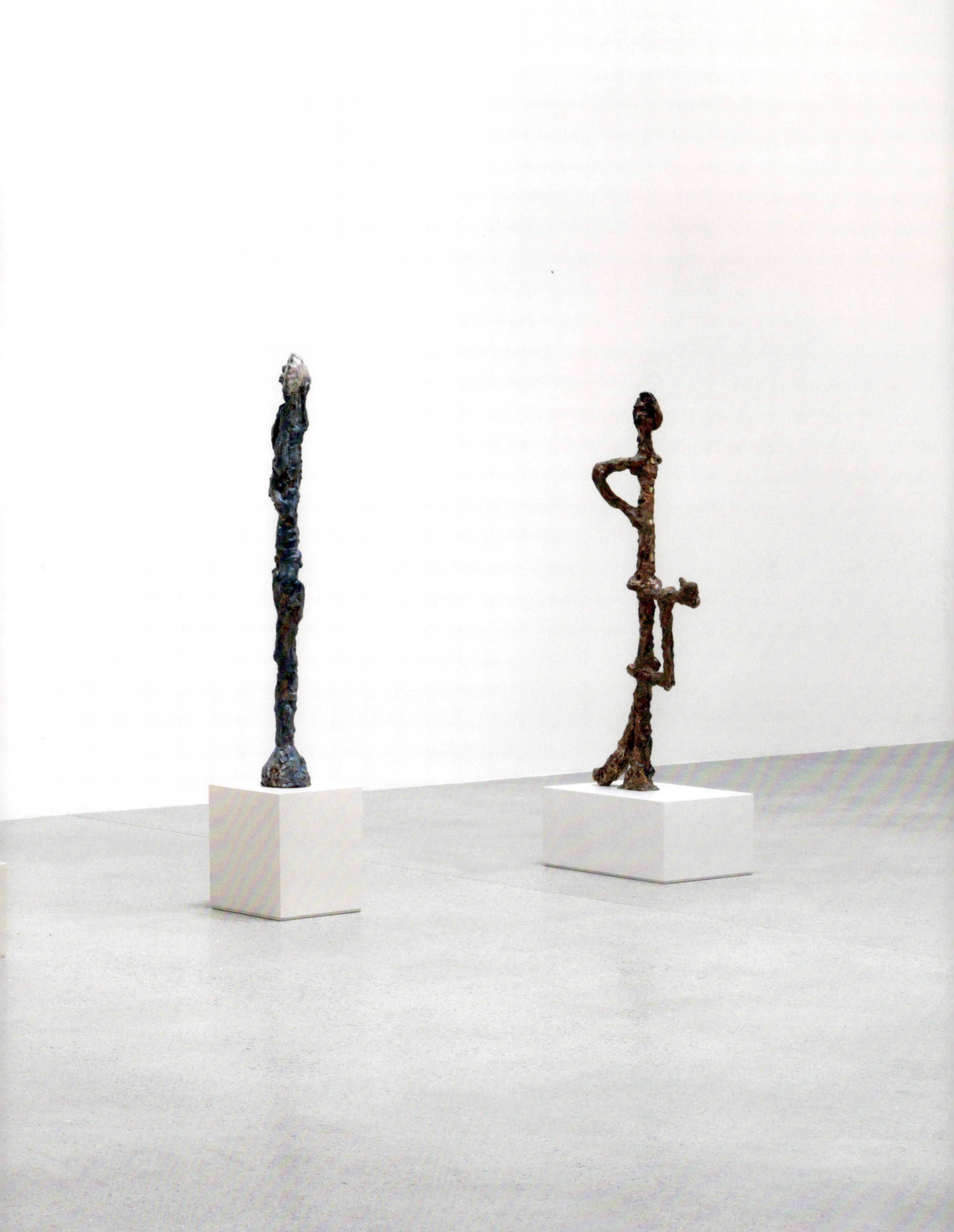

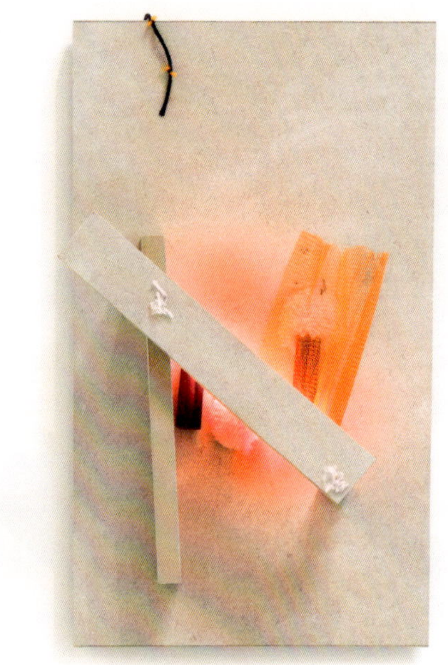

Shollage
2017

Los Hadeans (VI)
2017

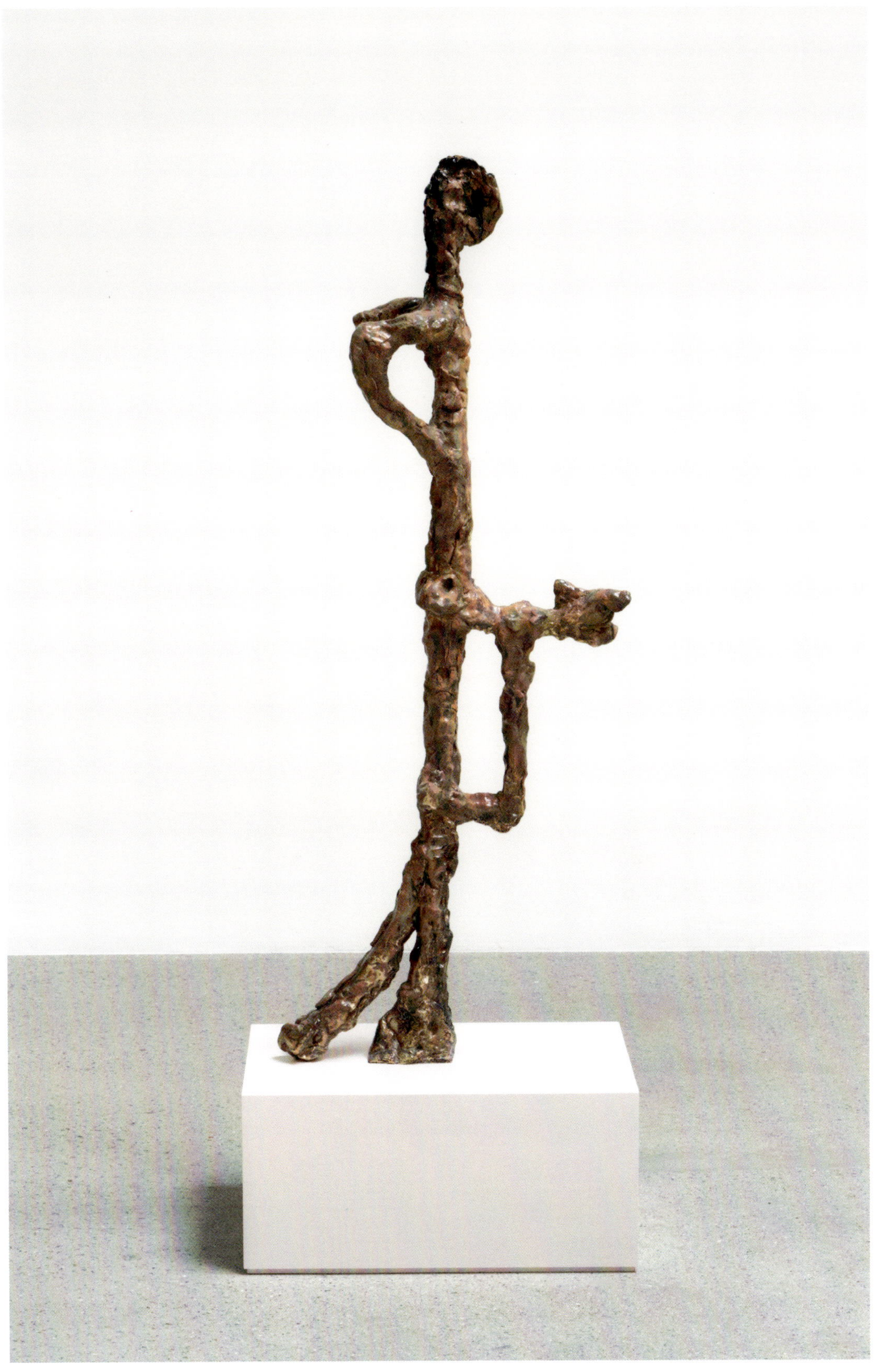

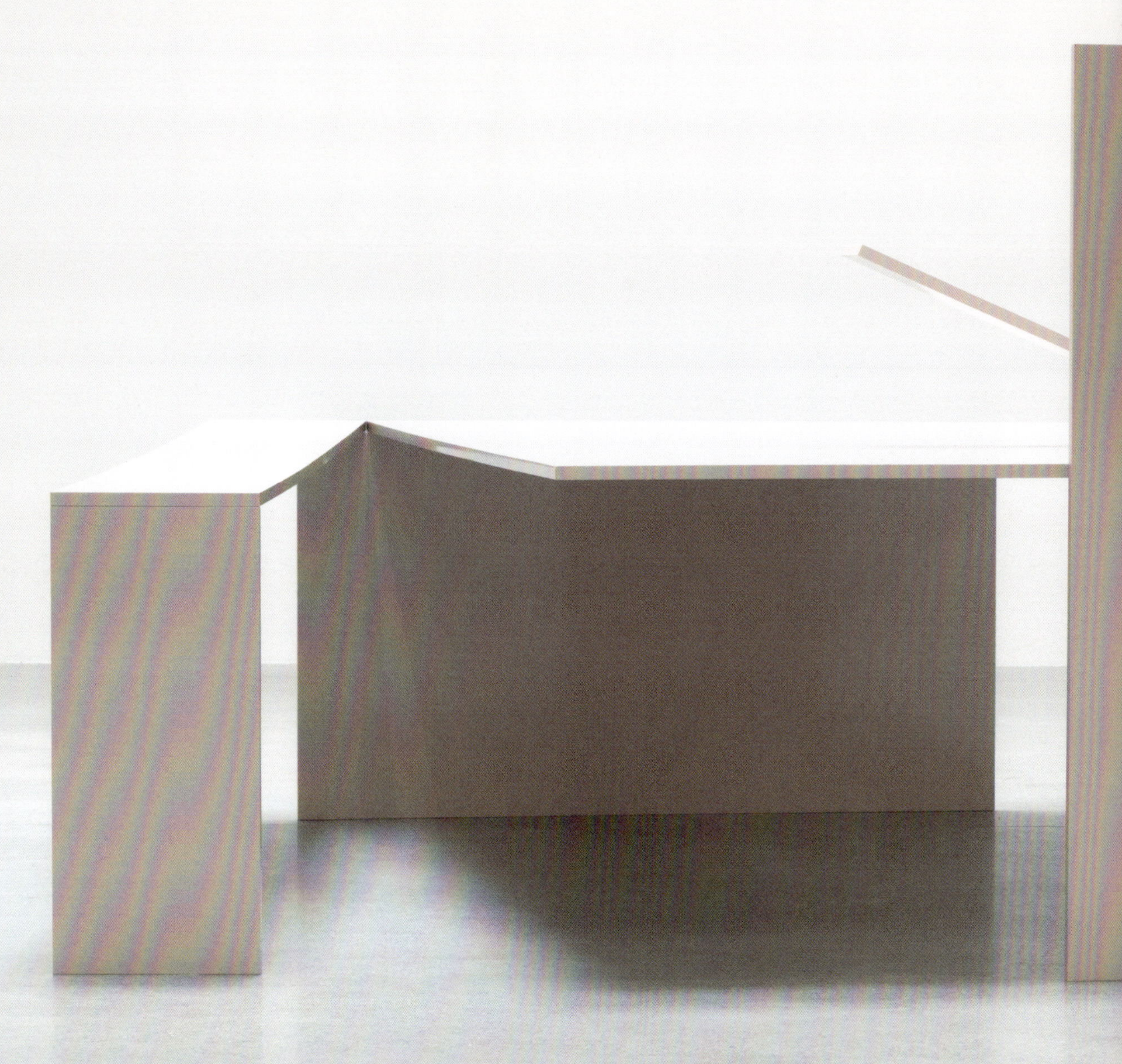

Let's All Chant (reprise)
2017

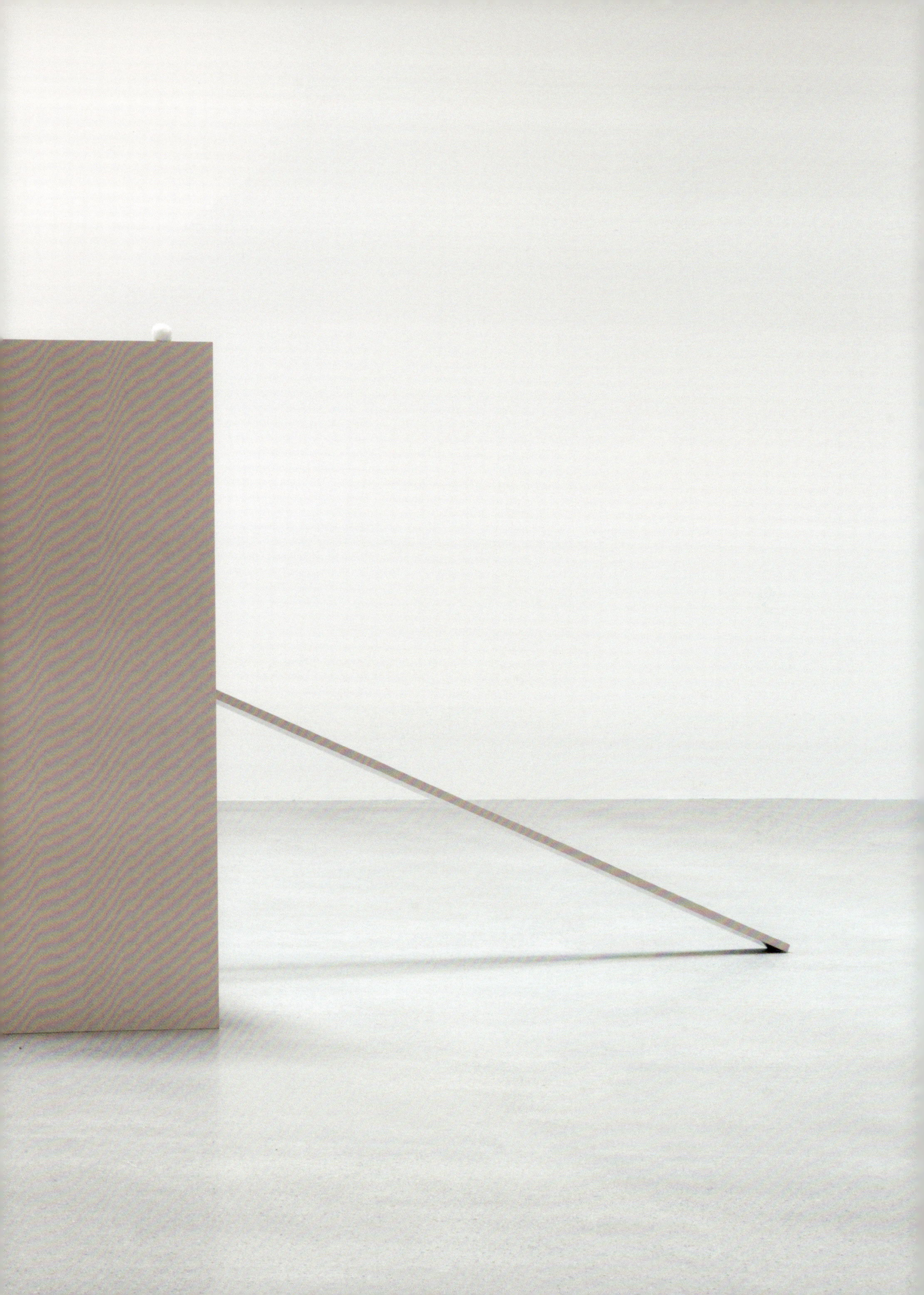

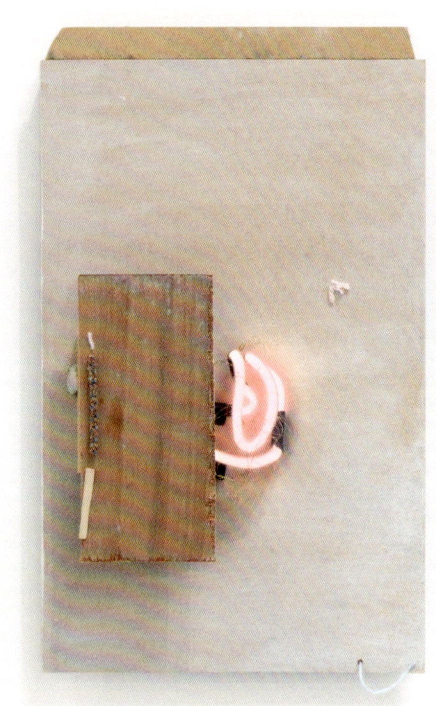

*Manliness without ostentation
(I learnt from what I heard
and can remember of my father)*
2017

The Three
2017

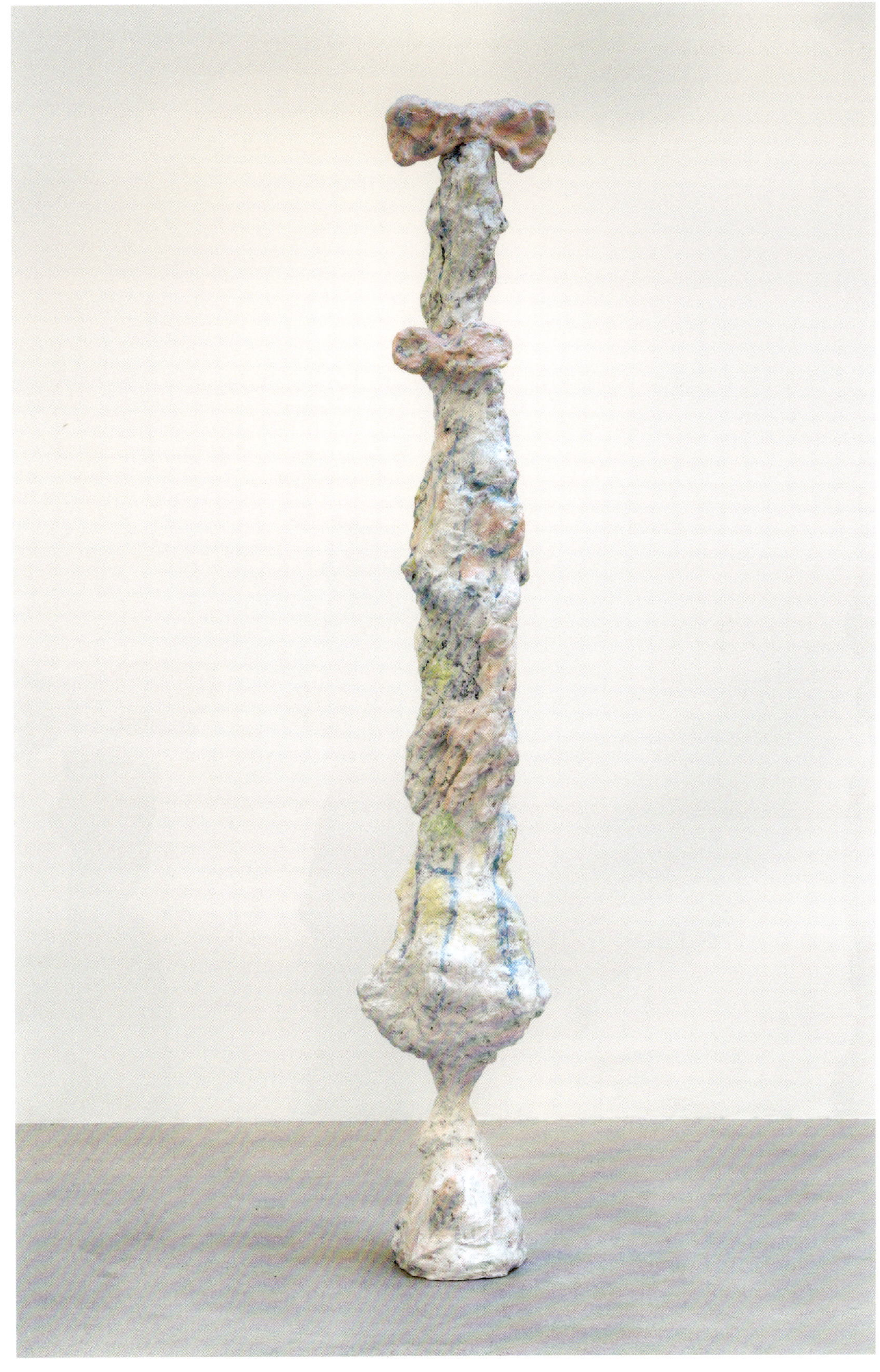

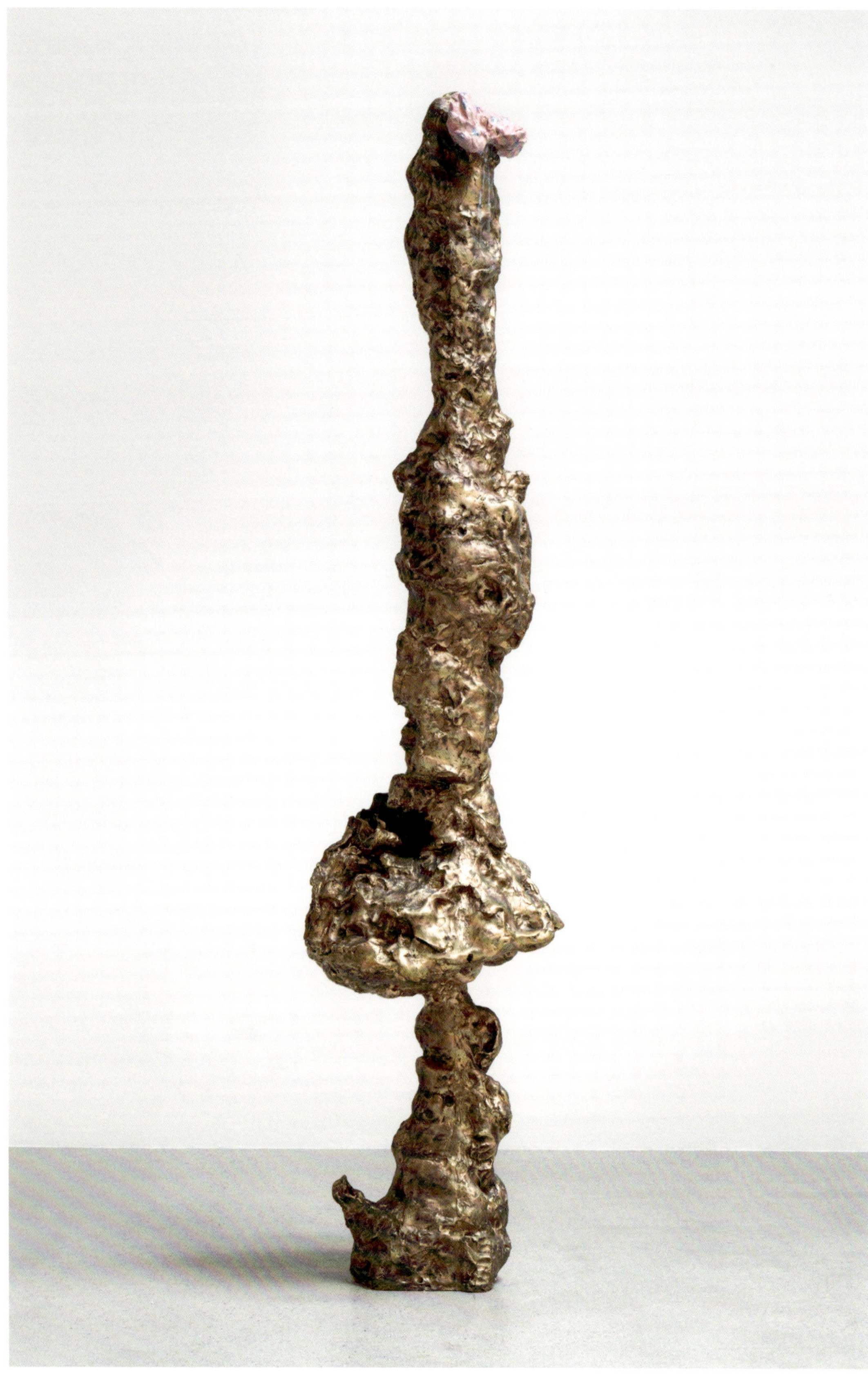

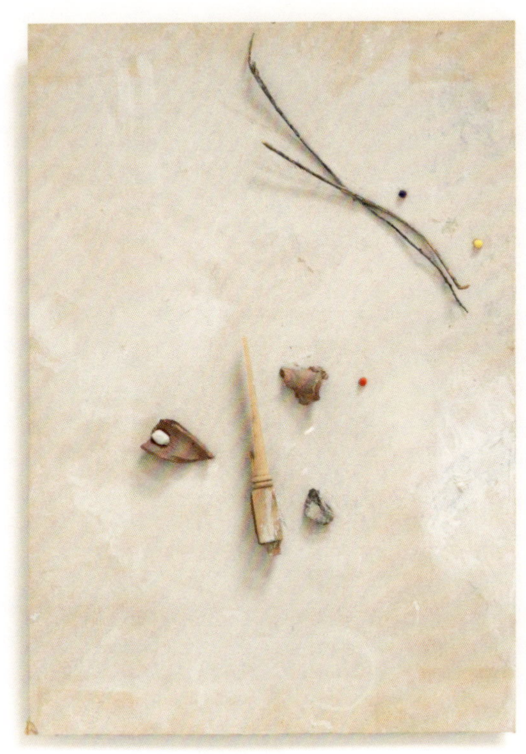

There's No Other Way
2010–17

Collage
2003

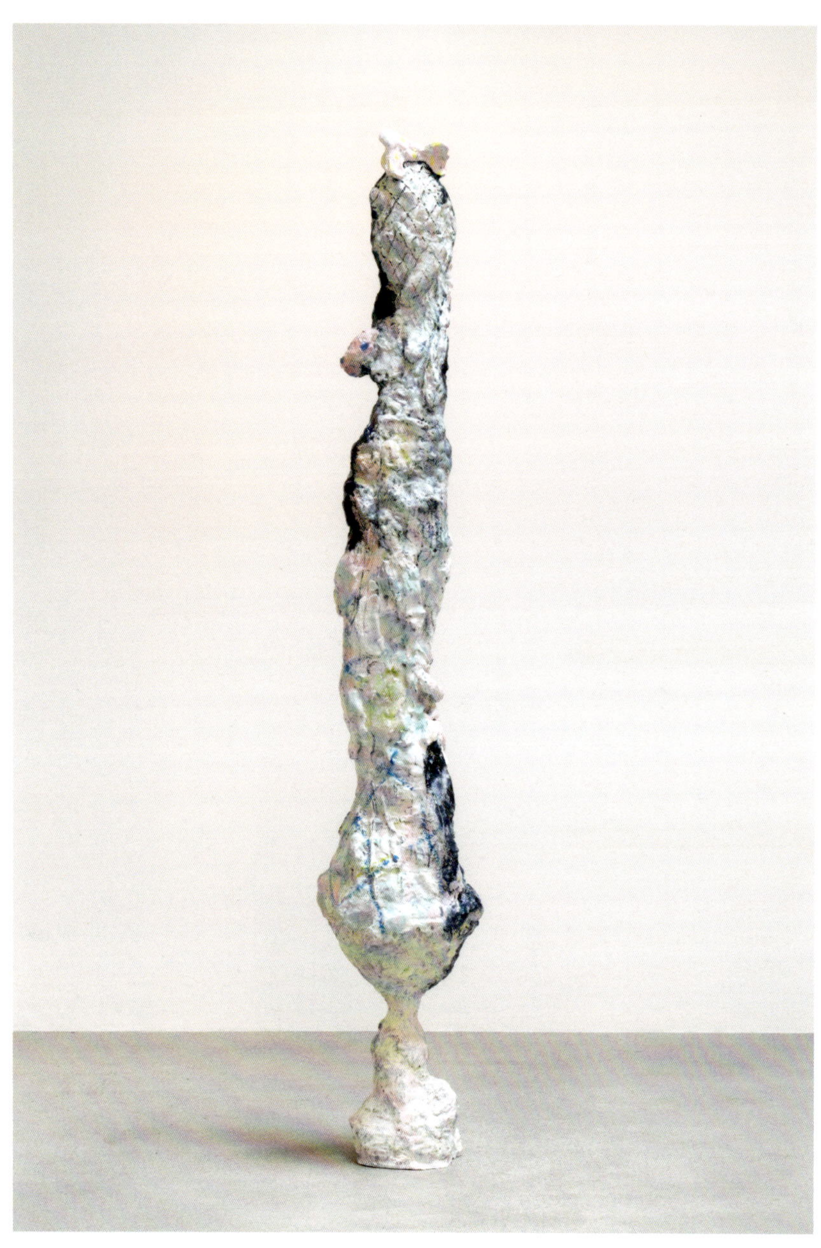

Aurelius
2017

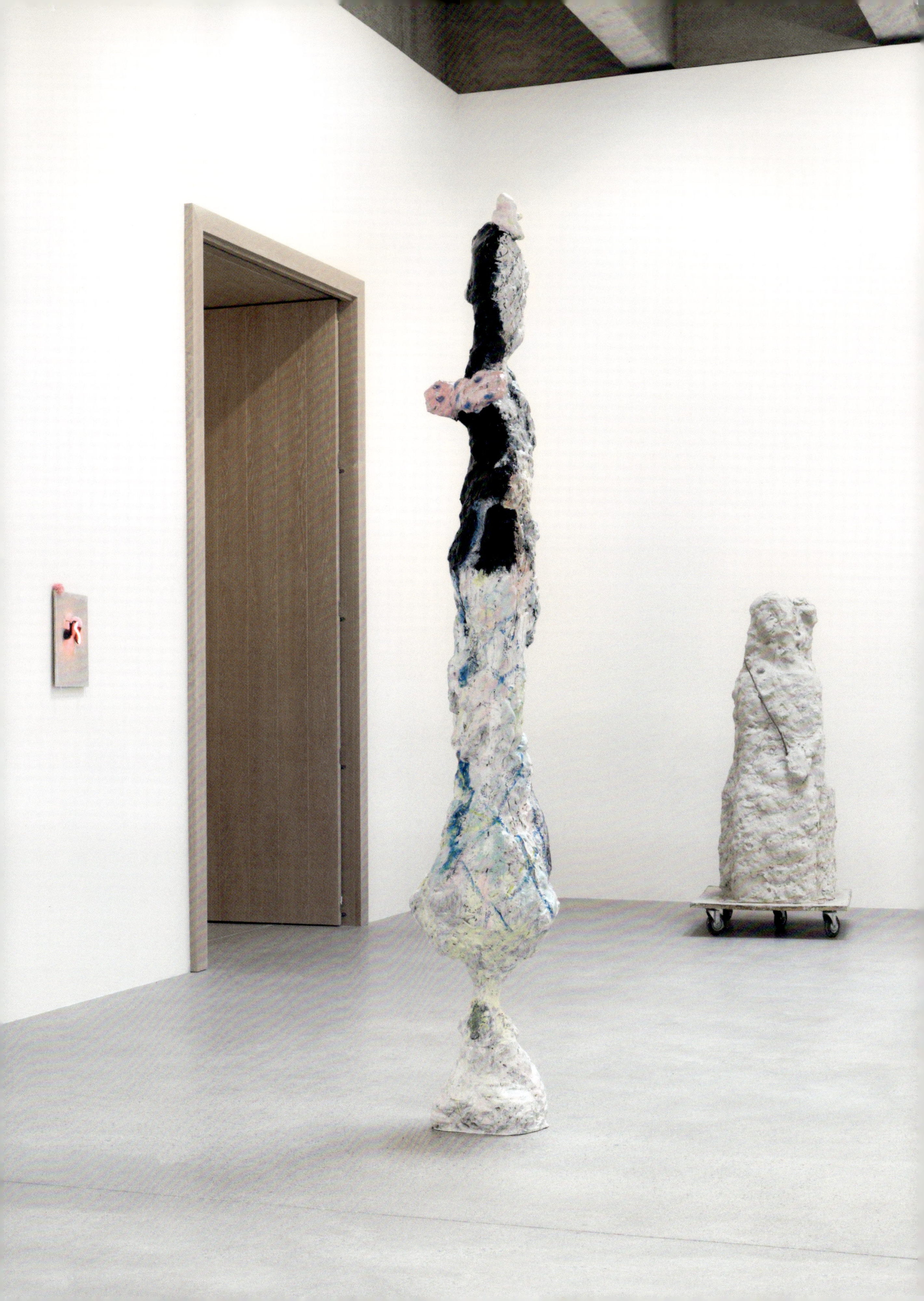

All that Heaven Allows
2017

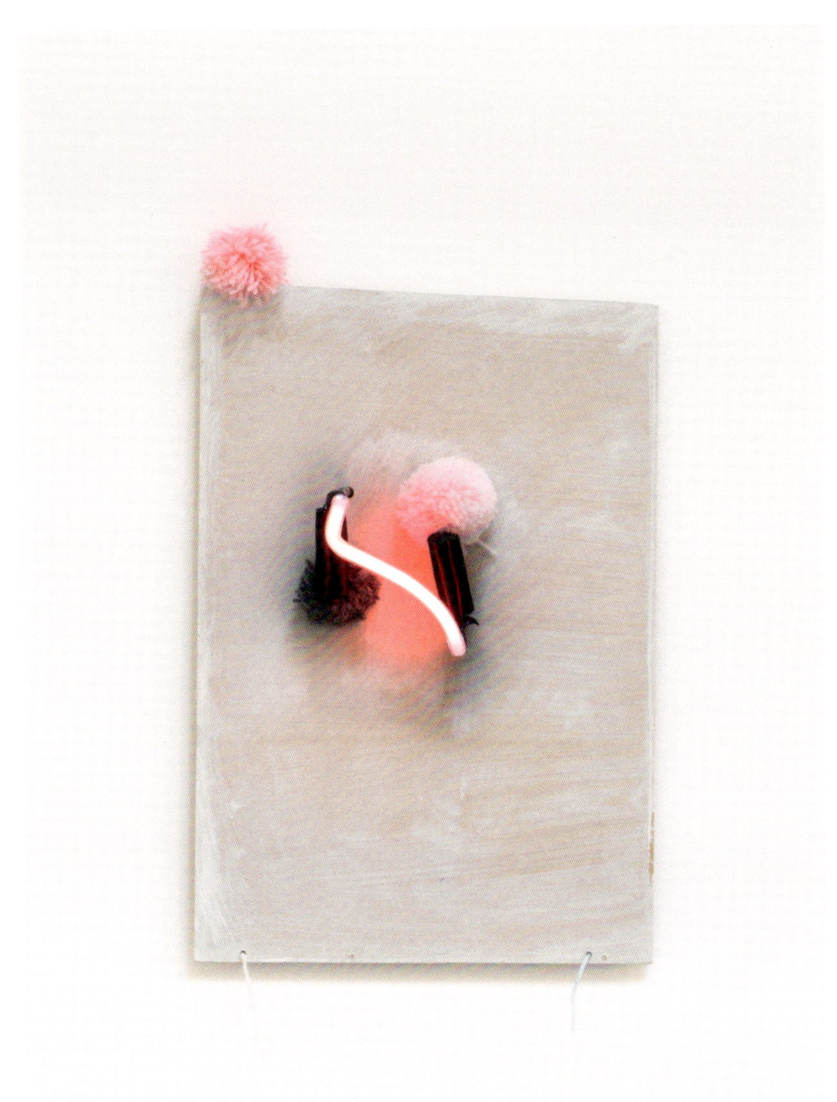

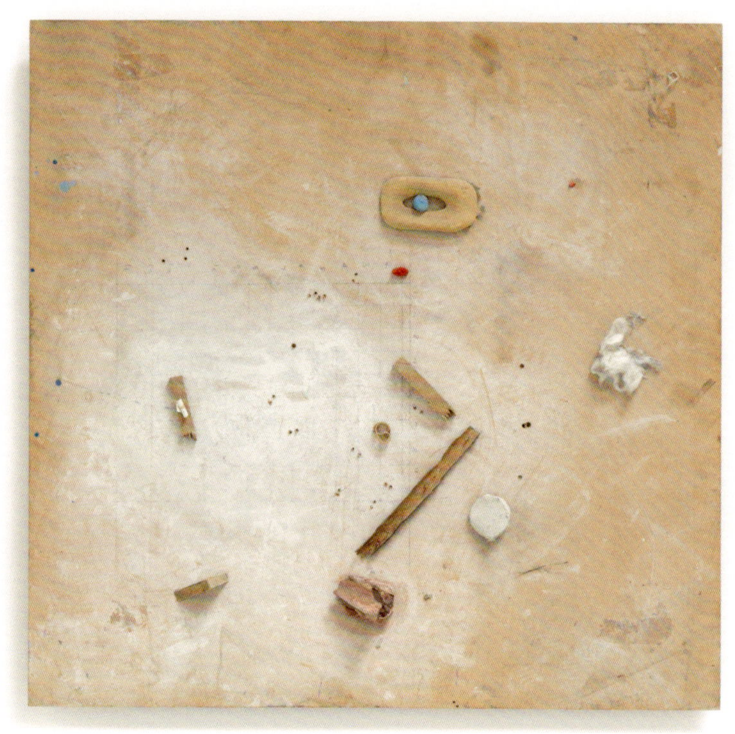

Homo Sapiens
2005

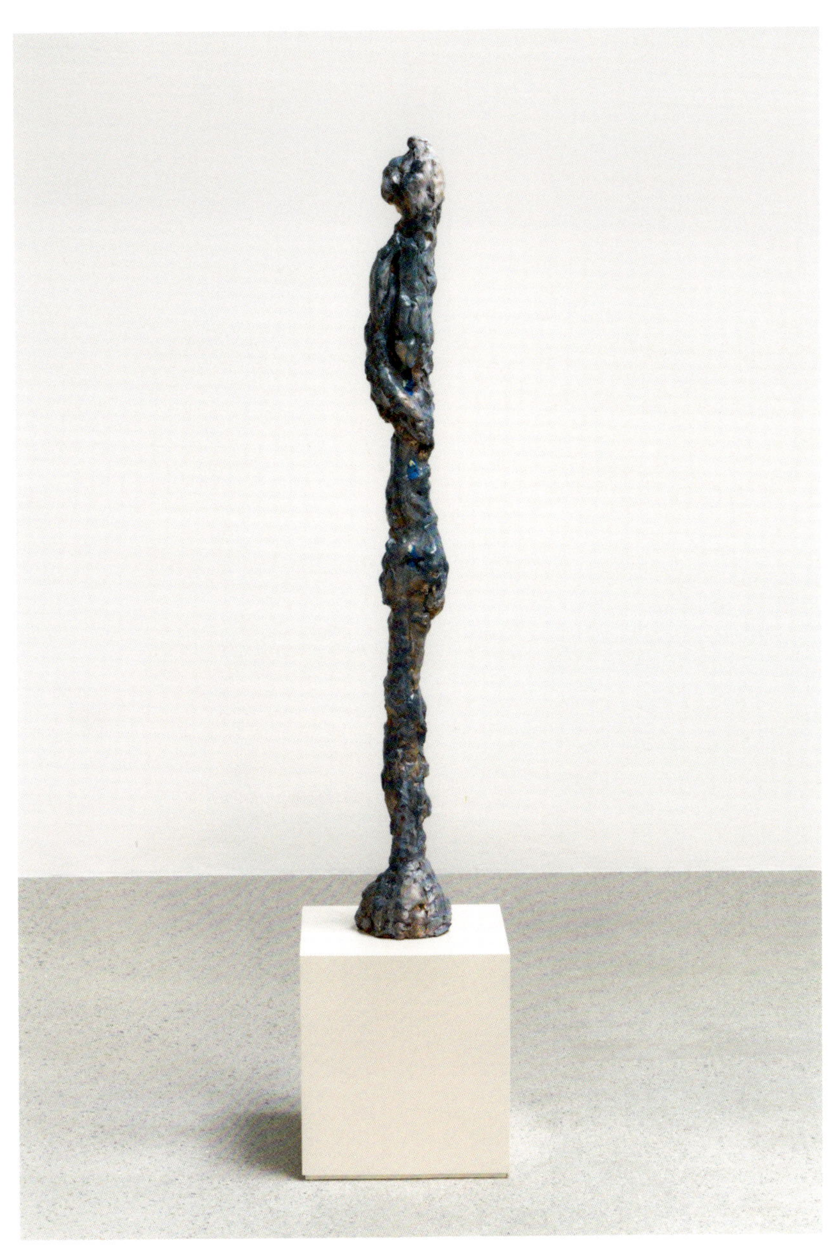

Los Hadeans (V)
2017

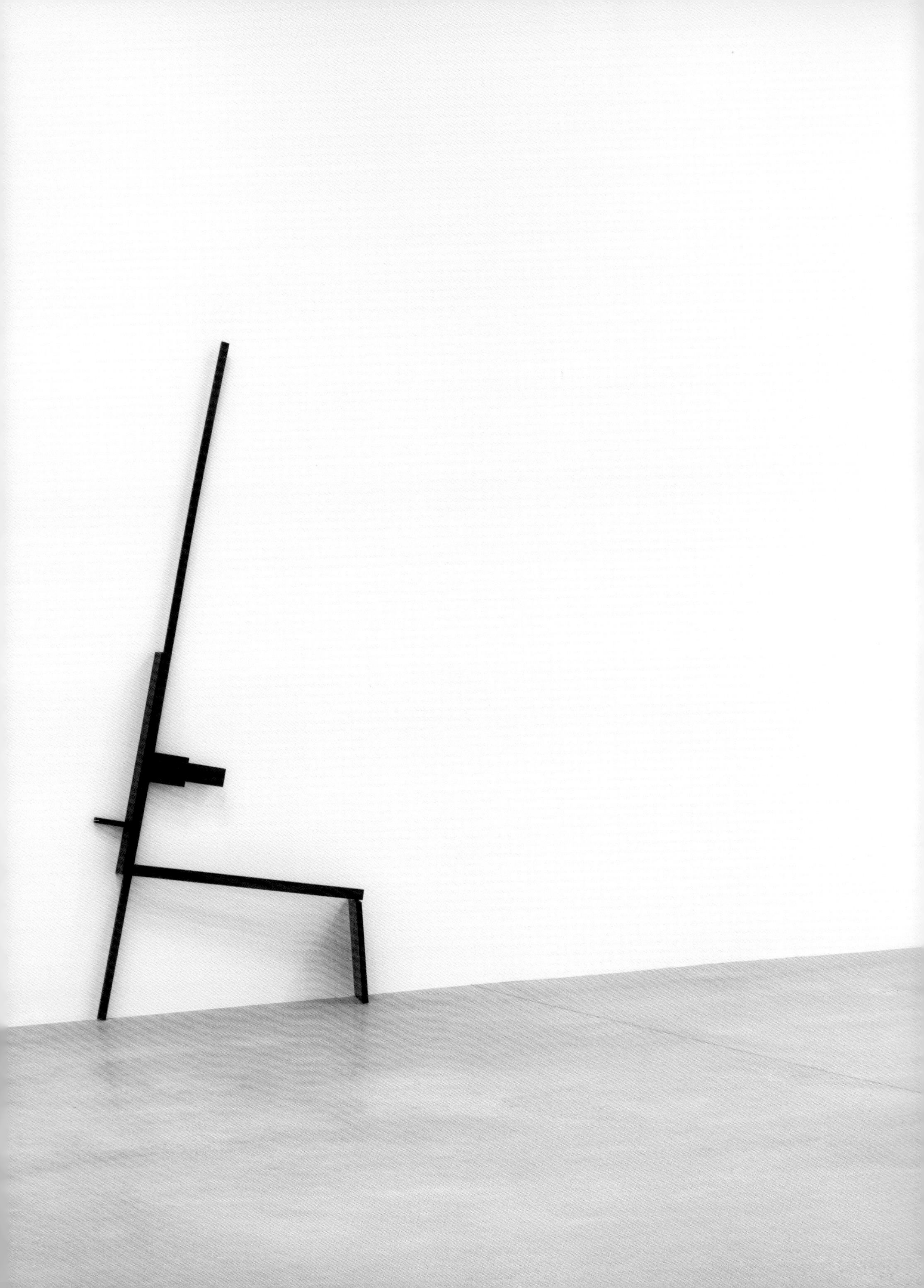

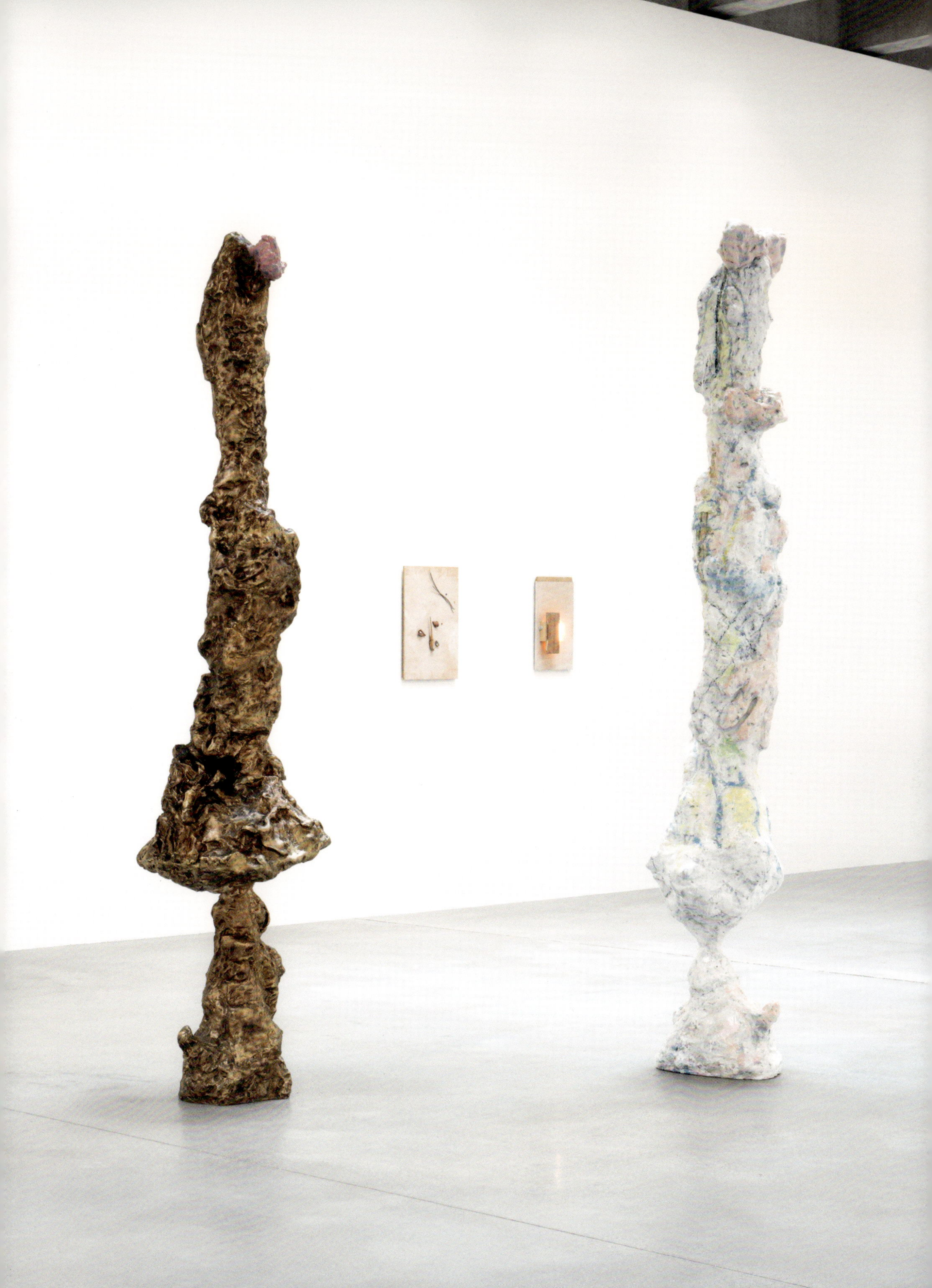

Rainer
2017

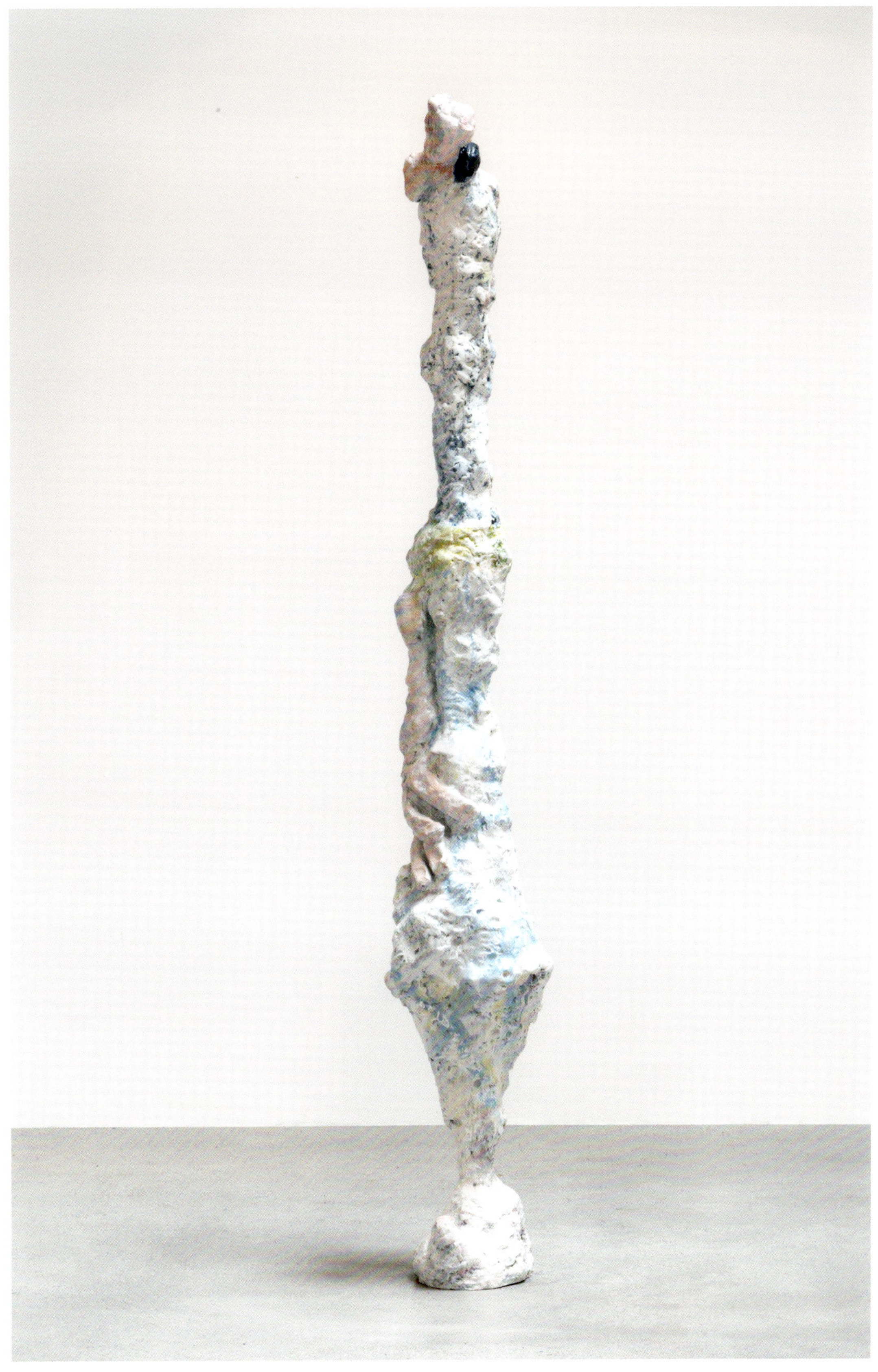

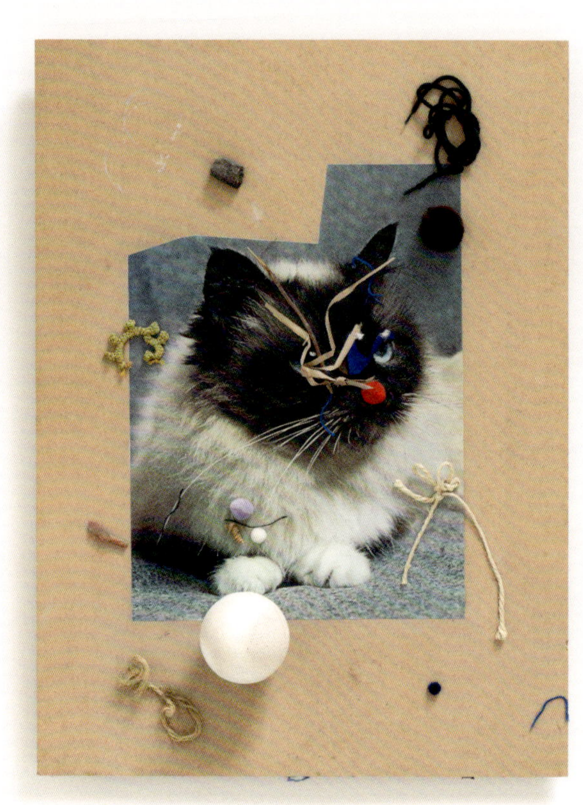

The Cat Stays in the Picture
2010

Telepathy
2017

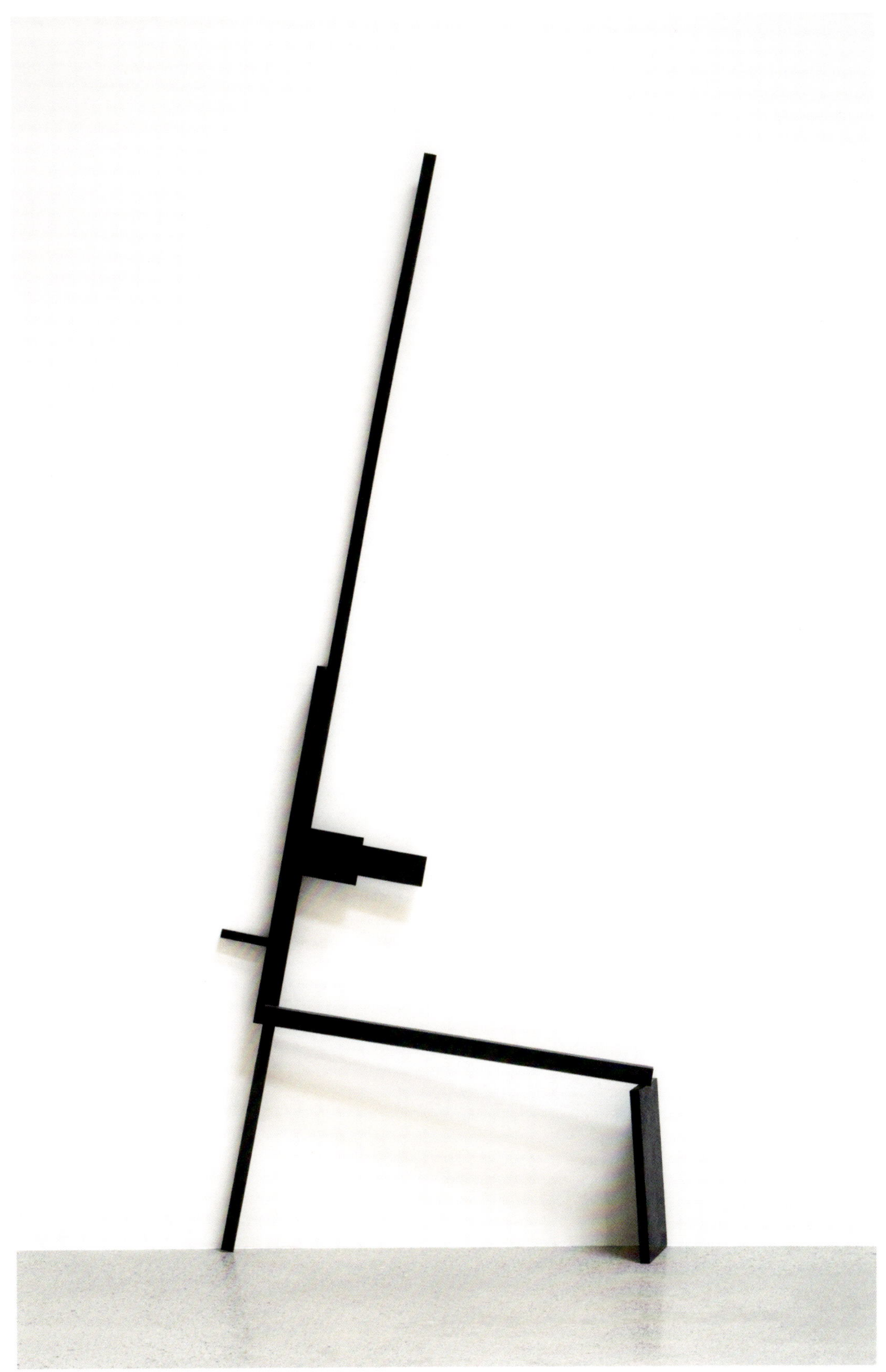

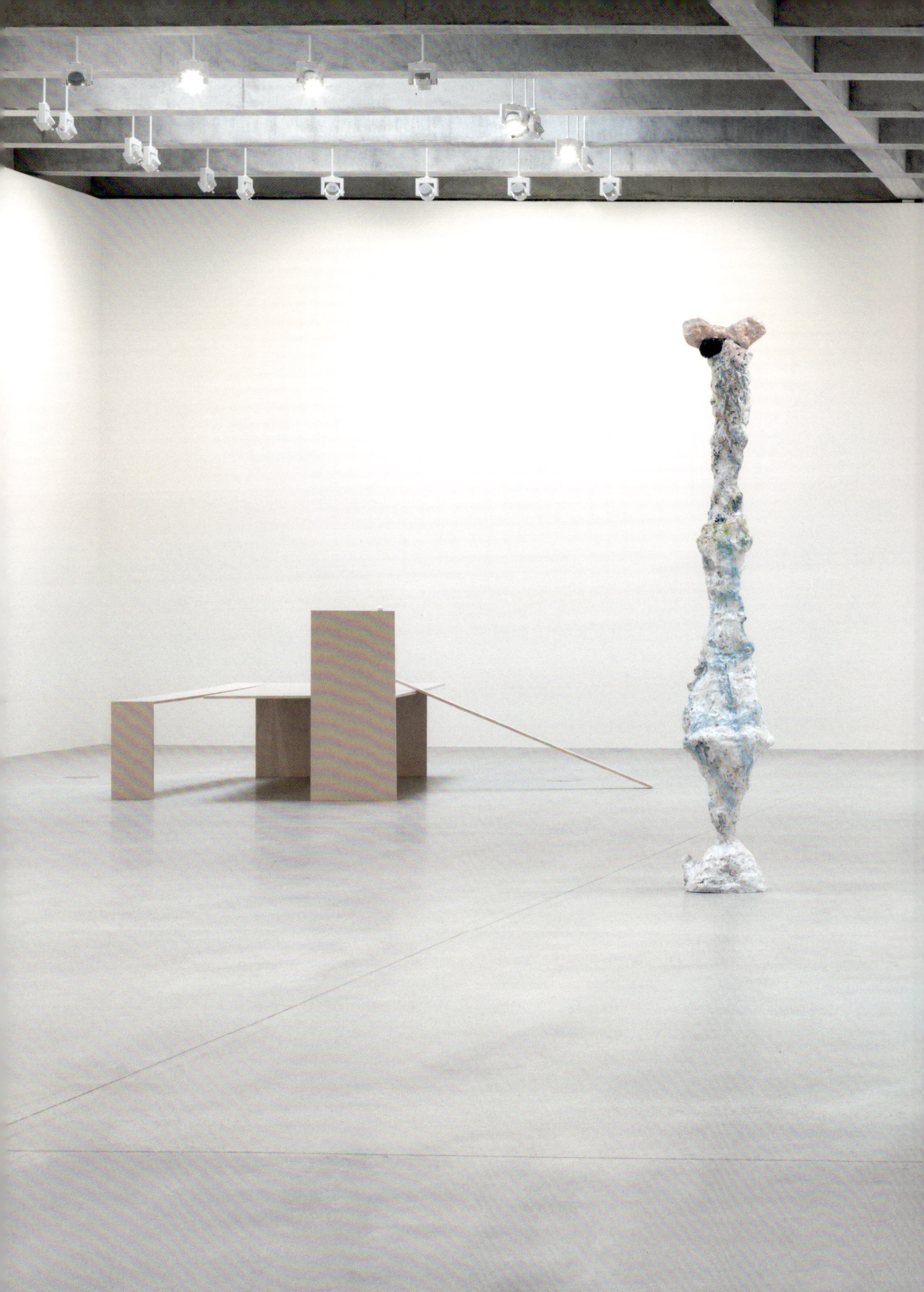

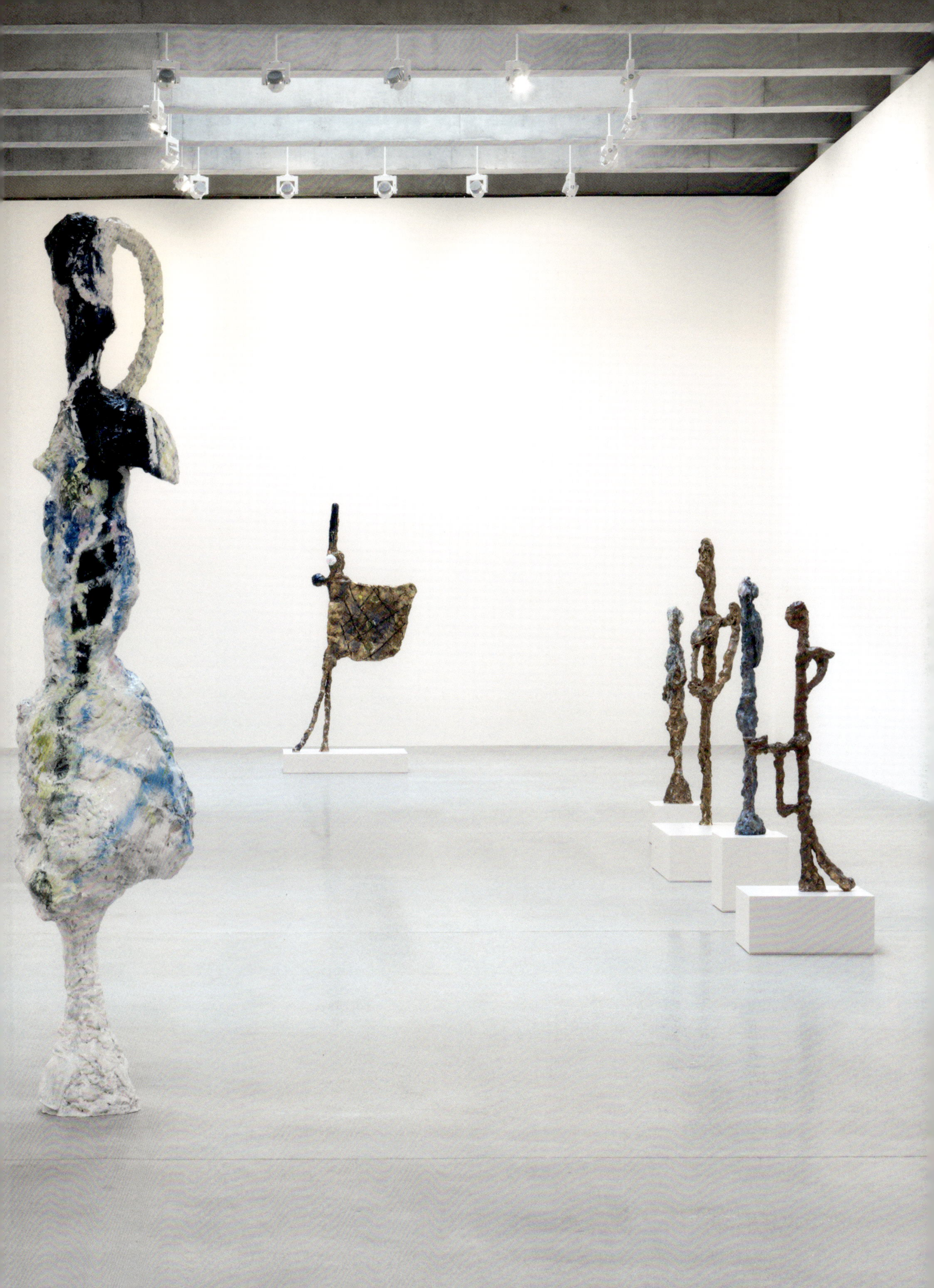